Peter McDonnell   Sarah Ackroyd

Messages

Teacher's Resource Pack

3

CAMBRIDGE
UNIVERSITY PRESS

CAMBRIDGE UNIVERSITY PRESS
Cambridge, New York, Melbourne, Madrid, Cape Town, Singapore, São Paulo

Cambridge University Press
The Edinburgh Building, Cambridge CB2 2RU, UK

www.cambridge.org
Information on this title: www.cambridge.org/9780521614368

First published 2006

Printed in the United Kingdom at the University Press, Cambridge.

A catalogue record for this publication is available from the British Library

ISBN-13 978-0-521-61436-8 Teacher's Resource Pack
ISBN-10 0-521-61436-8 Teacher's Resource Pack

ISBN-13 978-0-521-61433-7 Student's Book
ISBN-10 0-521-61433-3 Student's Book

ISBN-13 978-0-521-61434-4 Workbook with Audio CD / CD-ROM
ISBN-10 0-521-61434-1 Workbook with Audio CD / CD-ROM

ISBN-13 978-0-521-61435-1 Teacher's Book
ISBN-10 0-521-61435-X Teacher's Book

ISBN-13 978-0-521-61437-5 Class Cassettes
ISBN-10 0-521-61437-6 Class Cassettes

ISBN-13 978-0-521-61438-2 Class Audio CDs
ISBN-10 0-521-61438-4 Class Audio CDs

Contents

Introduction

The Teacher's Resource Pack for *Messages* Level 3 contains a range of photocopiable materials for you to use with your classes. It will help provide a complete set of materials for the classroom, with further resources available on the *Messages* website, www.cambridge.org/elt/messages

The Teacher's Resource Pack contains the following elements:

- Introduction with tests marking scheme
- Entry test and answer key
- Pattern drills
- Teaching notes and answer keys for the photocopiable activities
- Photocopiable communication activities and grammar exercises
- Module tests
- Final test
- Test answer keys

The contents are organised by these main areas, with each of the sections marked by a grey side label for easy reference.

Entry test

The entry test is for use at the beginning of the course and has been designed with two purposes. It can be used purely as a diagnostic entry test – there are straightforward language exercises to check how much students have retained from their previous learning – or it can be used to provide extra remedial practice.

Pattern drills

The pattern drills are designed to give students clearly staged practice of formulating newly learnt structures orally, thereby helping them to gain confidence before attempting to use the structures in a freer context. There is a drill for every key area of language taught in the course and some steps contain two drills. You may therefore wish to use them before the *Use what you know* activities in the corresponding steps. The Teacher's Book notes indicate where we would suggest using them in each case. Alternatively, you may wish to use them at a later stage as revision.

Recordings of the pattern drills are on the Class CDs/cassettes, and can be found in the position where the Teacher's Book notes recommend using them. The example sentence is recorded twice so that students can hear it with the response and then formulate it themselves. In all the pattern drills, there is a brief pause between the prompt and the response for you to pause the CD and allow students to say the sentence before they hear it.

Teaching notes for the photocopiable activities

These contain clear step-by-step instructions for all the activities. In addition, there are answers for the communication activities where relevant and answers for all of the grammar practice exercises.

Photocopiable communication activities and grammar exercises

The communication activities reflect the key grammar and/or vocabulary in each unit. They are designed to activate new language in a communicative context. They cover a range of fun and motivating activity types, for example, board games, quizzes, information gap activities, descriptions, etc.

The grammar exercises cover specific areas of the key grammar from each unit. They are intended for fast finishers or students who need extra practice.

Mixed-ability classes: if you have a mixed-ability class and your students need further remedial practice, please log onto our website www.cambridge.org/elt/messages where you can download easier grammar exercises. There are four of these exercises for every unit in the book.

Module tests

Please see page 5 for a full marking scheme.

This section contains six module tests. Each of the tests covers one module (two units) in the Student's Book.

Each test consists of six parts:

Grammar (20 marks): this is divided into two sections (a and b), with ten marks each. Activity types vary, but include:

- Completing discrete, gapped sentences by selecting one word from three choices provided or by choosing from words in a box. Both of these activities are designed to test understanding of key language at sentence level.
- Writing the correct verb forms from a list of infinitives, or completing sentences using the correct tense, for example. This part is designed to test students' knowledge and use of key verb forms they have studied.
- Rewriting sentences from active to passive, or from direct to reported speech, for example.

Vocabulary (20 marks): is divided into two or three sections (a and b / a, b, c) with five or ten marks each. Activity types vary, but include:

- Completing discrete, gapped sentences by selecting one word from three choices provided or by choosing from words in a box. These test students' ability to use new vocabulary in the correct contexts.

- Spelling a word by placing the letters in the correct order, or completing the missing letters of a word after reading a clue. Both of these activities test students' ability to spell and to recognise words on an individual level.

Reading (10 marks): in each of these sections there is one or more texts with comprehension questions. These may be true/false statements, matching exercises, or selecting an answer from three choices provided, for example. They are designed to test students on the type of sub-skills practised in the Student's Book, for example, reading for specific information, or gist.

Writing (10 marks): in this section students do a short piece of creative writing, for example they write a reply to a prompt such as an email or letter from an imaginary penfriend and must include specific topics in their answers.

Listening (10 marks): the listening section is divided into two sections. Students listen to two extracts, each with five questions: a dialogue, a monologue or several speakers, which is played at least twice. Students are tested on their general understanding, for example, the topics discussed or the speakers' attitudes, as well as their ability to listen for specific information. They may be required to answer specific questions, fill in questions with missing information, choose the correct picture from three choices provided, match speakers to pictures or choose from true/false statements.

NB The recordings for the listening tests are on the Class Cassettes/CDs, at the end of each module.

Speaking (10 marks): this section is divided into two sections (a and b). In part a, students are required to answer specific questions asked by you. These always start with greetings, and are followed by questions based on topics and language covered in the modules. They are designed to help students activate the language they have learnt and demonstrate their knowledge of the key vocabulary and grammar. In part b students work with another student to complete a designated task based on prompt cards. The speaking section of the test includes both the instructions for the teachers and the prompt cards for the students. In most cases you will only need to copy one page for each pair of students.

Final test

The final test has the same format and marks available as the modular tests, but tests language from all parts of the course. As its name suggests, it is designed to be done upon completion of the course, and may therefore be used as an end-of-year test.

Examinations

The modular tests and final test of *Messages* have been designed to provide useful preparation for students taking public examinations such as Cambridge ESOL KET and Trinity Integrated Skills.

Test keys

These are positioned at the end of each test and include tapescripts for the listening tests.

Test marking scheme

The answer key to the entry test is on page 10. The marking scheme is straightforward and the number of marks awarded is written at the end of each exercise.

Each of the modular tests and the final test have six components and there are 80 marks available. Each test follows the same format:

Section 1	Grammar	20 marks
Section 2	Vocabulary	20 marks
Section 3	Reading	10 marks
Section 4	Writing	10 marks
Section 5	Listening	10 marks
Section 6	Speaking	10 marks

How to mark Section 4 Writing

Each item has a maximum of five marks, giving a total of ten marks. Marks should be awarded according to two main criteria:

- Relevant content. Has the student answered the question fully and included all the given topics? (5 marks)
- Appropriate use of grammar and vocabulary, including spelling. (5 marks)

How to mark Section 6 Speaking

In each of the two sections, give each student a mark based on overall performance. Marks should be awarded according to two main criteria:

- Task completion: have they included the main points in their prompts? Have their responses been relevant? Have they managed to communicate their ideas successfully, without too many misunderstandings? (5 marks)
- Appropriate use of grammar and vocabulary. (5 marks)

In section b, where the two students talk to each other, it is important to judge each separately: for example, if Student B is weak, this should not affect the mark of a stronger Student A.

The marks should be recorded on the Listening page of each student's test in the box labelled 'Speaking'.

1 Grammar

Name ....

Class .... Date ....

a Complete the sentences. Circle the right answer: a, b or c.

0 A: ...... 's this?

   B: It's a dictionary.

   a Who (b) What   c Who's

1 Tom ...... often late for dinner.

   a are   b is   c am

2 Sara ...... speak French, but she speaks Spanish and English.

   a not   b don't   c doesn't

3 The book isn't as good ...... the film.

   a than   b as   c to

4 How ...... homework did you do yesterday?

   a much   b many   c long

5 There are ...... of parks in London.

   a many   b a lot   c much

6 ...... was very cold last night.

   a There   b They   c It

7 A: Did Ben go swimming on Monday?

   B. ....

   a Yes, he did.   b No, he doesn't.

   c Yes, he does.

8 Sorry we're late. We couldn't find ...... books.

   a their   b his   c our

9 Would you like ...... milk in your tea?

   a some   b a   c many

10 If we ...... time, we'll help you.

   a are having   b had   c have

   ☐ 10

b Complete the sentences using the correct form of the verbs in the box.

get   learn   go   ~~come~~   arrive   meet
listen   babysit   not remember
not believe   play

0 We'll buy you a pizza if you __come__ with us.

1 Sam .... to the radio when the phone rang.

2 Tom and Jess .... tennis yesterday.

3 We .... to the beach every weekend. It's great.

4 Are you busy this evening? Yes, I .... for my aunt.

5 I .... you! It's not true!

6 Next year I .... a new computer.

7 The Browns were watching television when John ....

8 Amy felt awful because she .... her father's birthday.

9 What .... you .... in geography at the moment?

10 See you tomorrow! I .... you at the bus stop.

   ☐ 10

Name ....

Class .... Date ....

c Complete the table with the comparative and superlative form of the adjectives.

Adjective	Comparative	Superlative
0 long	*longer than*	*the longest*
1 big	....	....
2 good	....	....
3 expensive	....	....
4 bad	....	....
5 important	....	....
6 friendly	....	....
7 nice	....	....
8 lazy	....	....
9 loud	....	....
10 angry	....	....

10

d Underline the right answer.

0 You <u>shouldn't</u> / must eat a lot of chocolate!

1 I must / can't play tennis at the moment because I broke my leg last week.

2 You mustn't / can't play with fire – it's very dangerous.

3 I really can / should go to bed earlier. I'm always so tired.

4 Dan should / can speak French very well.

5 You must / can see Penelope Cruz's new film. It's excellent.

6 I'm sorry but I can't / mustn't remember your name.

7 You should / shouldn't eat fast food. It's bad for you.

8 I don't think I must / can come to your party on Saturday.

9 You mustn't / must give Josh my phone number because I don't like him!

10 We can / should go now – it's midnight!

10

Grammar	40

2 Vocabulary

Name
Class   Date

a Complete the sentences. Circle the right answer: a, b or c.

0   Max fell in love _____ Chloe last year.

   a to   (b) with   c of

1   Turn left at the end _____ the street.

   a in   b of   c from

2   She's very _____ . She was the best in her class at school.

   a silly   b intelligent   c awful

3   What are you doing this _____ ?

   a night   b evening   c day

4   Good _____ with your exams. I'm sure you'll be fine.

   a chance   b lucky   c luck

5   I'm crazy _____ *Friends*. It's my favourite programme.

   a for   b about   c with

6   They're going to France next week. They're _____ the ferry.

   a going   b getting   c having

7   I can't give you the photos. My _____ isn't working.

   a mouse   b printer   c screen

8   I'm going to buy some bread at the _____ .

   a baker's   b post office   c chemist's

9   The _____ is changing. I'm sure the summers are getting hotter.

   a climate   b air   c soil

10 Excuse me, can you tell me the _____ to the swimming-pool?

   a road   b street   c way

[ ] 10

b What are these things? Write the names.

0   We've got a new D_VD_ p_layer_ . Do you want to watch *The Incredibles*?

1   My mum bought me an electric t _ _ _ _ _ _ _ _ after my last visit to the dentist.

2   My grandmother didn't have a w _ _ _ _ _ _ m _ _ _ _ _ _ , so she spent hours washing everyone's clothes.

3   A: Is there any milk?

   B: Yes, it's in the f _ _ _ _ _ .

4   We often use a c_ _ _ _ _ c_ _ _ to pay for things when we go shopping.

5   Put the potatoes in the m _ _ _ _ _ _ _ _ for five minutes and they'll be ready. It's very quick.

6   James loves taking photos and he always has his d _ _ _ _ _ _ c _ _ _ _ _ with him.

7   I usually have a s _ _ _ _ _ in the morning before I get dressed.

8   The t _ _ _ _ _ _ _ _ is ringing. Perhaps it's John.

9   I often listen to music on the s _ _ _ _ _ when I do my homework.

10 I always take my s_ _ _ _ _ _ _ _ when I go to the beach – I love surfing.

[ ] 10

c Complete the sentences with an adjective from the box.

Name ....

Class .... Date ....

| ~~strange~~ dangerous easy expensive high |
| tall kind boring funny cheap difficult |

0 I had a _____*strange*_____ dream last night and I couldn't sleep.

1 $5 for a pair of shoes? That's so _____ !

2 I thought the maths test was really _____ . I couldn't answer any of the questions.

3 Michael's quite _____ – he's 1m 85.

4 You shouldn't swim in the sea here. It's too _____ .

5 I always have a good time with Natalie. She's really _____ .

6 I couldn't buy you a present yesterday because everything was so _____

and I didn't have much money.

7 Matt is very _____ – he's always happy to help.

8 How _____ is Mount Everest?

9 A: What's 2 + 2?

   B: Oh, that's too _____ . Ask me something harder!

10 This book is really _____ . I go to sleep every time I start reading it.

`10`

d Jobs. Label each picture.

0 _____*teacher*_____   3 _____   6 _____   9 _____

1 _____   4 _____   7 _____   10 _____

2 _____   5 _____   8 _____

`10`

| Vocabulary | 40 |

| Test total | 80 |

1 Grammar

a 1 b   2 c   3 b   4 a   5 b   6 c   7 a   8 c   9 a   10 c

b 1 was listening   2 played   3 go   4 'm/am babysitting   5 don't believe
6 'll/will get / 'm/am going to get / 'm/am getting   7 arrived
8 didn't remember   9 are ... learning   10 'll meet

c 1 bigger, the biggest   2 better, the best   3 more expensive, the most expensive
4 worse, the worst   5 more important, the most important   6 friendlier, the
friendliest   7 nicer, the nicest   8 lazier, the laziest   9 louder, the loudest
10 angrier, the angriest

d 1 can't   2 mustn't   3 should   4 can   5 must   6 can't   7 shouldn't   8 can
9 mustn't   10 should

2 Vocabulary

a 1 b   2 b   3 b   4 c   5 b   6 b   7 b   8 a   9 a   10 c

b 1 toothbrush   2 washing machine   3 fridge   4 credit card   5 microwave
6 digital camera   7 shower   8 telephone   9 stereo   10 surfboard

c 1 cheap   2 difficult   3 tall   4 dangerous   5 funny   6 expensive   7 kind
8 high   9 easy   10 boring

d 1 waitress   2 builder   3 pilot   4 secretary   5 shop assistant   6 farmer
7 taxi driver   8 film director   9 disc jockey   10 mechanic

Unit 1 Step 2  Class CD 1 Track 7

1 **Present continuous: questions**

 Listen to the example, then ask questions about what the people are doing at the moment.

Jay's laughing. (Why)
Why's he laughing?

I'm watching TV. (What)
What are you watching?

Ana and Penny are eating. (What)
What are they eating?

Charlie's going out. (Where)
Where's he going?

I'm phoning someone. (Who)
Who are you phoning?

Unit 1 Step 2 Class CD 1 Track 8

2 **Present simple and present continuous**

Listen to the example, then say what they usually do.

Lucy's having spaghetti for lunch. (a sandwich)
She usually has a sandwich.

Ana's writing a letter. (emails)
She usually writes emails.

My brother's reading the newspaper. (magazines)
He usually reads magazines.

I'm going to a rugby match. (football matches)
I usually go to football matches.

We're listening to classical music. (pop music)
We usually listen to pop music.

Unit 2 Step 1  Class CD 1 Track 12

1 **Past simple: irregular verbs**

 Listen to the example, then make sentences about yesterday.

Charlie gets the bus to school.
He got the bus to school yesterday.

I don't get up early.
I didn't get up early yesterday.

Danny buys a magazine every week.
He bought a magazine yesterday.

I have a shower every day.
I had a shower yesterday.

Jay's dad doesn't drive to work.
He didn't drive to work yesterday.

Unit 2 Step 1 Class CD 1 Track 14

2 **Past simple: questions**

Listen to the example, then ask questions about what the people did.

Charlie got up late. (What time)
What time did he get up?

Ana went to the police station. (Why)
Why did she go to the police station?

We saw someone famous. (Who)
Who did you see?

Penny left early. (When)
When did she leave?

Tim and Penny bought a new computer. (Where)
Where did they buy it?

Marcus knew all the answers. (How)
How did he know all the answers?

PATTERN DRILLS

Unit 2 Step 2  Class CD 1 Track 18

Past simple and past continuous

 Listen to the example, then say what each student was doing when the teacher came into the classroom.

What were Sam and Nick doing when the teacher came in? (talk)
They were talking.

What were you doing when the teacher came in? (look out of the window)
I was looking out of the window.

What was Lucy doing when the teacher came in? (laugh)
She was laughing.

What were Rose and Paul doing when the teacher came in? (play cards)
They were playing cards.

What were you and Maria doing when the teacher came in? (read)
We were reading.

Unit 3 Step 1 Class CD 1 Track 23

Comparatives

Listen to the example, then make comparative sentences.

Cassettes are cheaper than CDs. (expensive)
CDs are more expensive than cassettes.

England's colder than Morocco. (hot)
Morocco's hotter than England.

Russia's bigger than Italy. (small)
Italy's smaller than Russia.

Ana's shyer than Lizzie. (confident)
Lizzie's more confident than Ana.

Painting's more difficult than drawing. (easy)
Drawing's easier than painting.

Unit 3 Step 2  Class CD 1 Track 27

as ... as

Listen to the example, then make sentences with *as ... as*

The Seine is a long river. (the Nile)
It isn't as long as the Nile.

Tessa's very fast. (Megan)
She isn't as fast as Megan.

The Red Hot Chilli Peppers are good. (Coldplay)
They aren't as good as Coldplay.

Michael's very tall. (Danny)
He isn't as tall as Danny.

English is difficult. (Chinese)
It isn't as difficult as Chinese.

Unit 4 Step 1  Class CD 1 Track 32

Suggestions

Listen to the example, then make suggestions.

Do you want to have a picnic? (How about)
Yes! How about having a picnic?

Do you want to meet at the cinema? (Why don't we)
Yes! Why don't we meet at the cinema?

Do you want to watch TV? (Shall we)
Yes! Shall we watch TV?

Do you want to buy some postcards? (Let's)
Yes! Let's buy some postcards.

Do you want to go shopping? (Shall we)
Yes! Shall we go shopping?

Do you want to have lunch? (Why don't we)
Yes! Why don't we have lunch?

Unit 4 Step 2

1 *too much / too many*

🔊 Listen to the example, then make sentences with *There's too much* or *There are too many*.

cars
There are too many cars.

pollution
There's too much pollution.

buildings
There are too many buildings.

tourists
There are too many tourists.

traffic
There's too much traffic.

people
There are too many people.

Unit 4 Step 2

2 *not enough*

🔊 Listen to the example, then make sentences with *There isn't enough* or *There aren't enough*.

fruit juice
There isn't enough fruit juice.

butter
There isn't enough butter.

eggs
There aren't enough eggs.

coffee
There isn't enough coffee.

milk
There isn't enough milk.

tomatoes
There aren't enough tomatoes.

Unit 5 Step 1

1 Present continuous used for future arrangements

🔊 Listen to the example, then ask questions about the people's arrangements.

I'm having lunch with Tom. (What time)
What time are you having lunch?

Len and Clara are getting married? (When)
When are they getting married?

Tessa's having a party. (Why)
Why is she having a party?

I'm playing tennis with Tom tomorrow. (Where)
Where are you playing tennis?

Charlie's going out tonight. (What time)
What time is he going out?

Ana and Lizzie are going shopping. (When)
When are they going shopping?

Unit 5 Step 1

2 *Going to* used for intentions

🔊 What are these people going to do? Listen to the example and make sentences.

Lizzie and Martin / watch a film.
Lizzie and Martin are going to watch a film.

Ana / have a shower.
Ana's going to have a shower.

Mark / do his homework.
Mark's going to do his homework.

I / tidy my room.
I'm going to tidy my room.

Tim and Penny / buy a new car
Tim and Penny are going to buy a new car.

My sister / phone her boyfriend.
My sister's going to phone her boyfriend.

Unit 5 Step 2

Will for making offers

 Listen to the example, then make offers.

I'm cold! (close the door)
I'll close the door.

This bag's very heavy! (carry it)
I'll carry it.

I can't do this exercise! (help you)
I'll help you.

The phone's ringing! (answer it)
I'll answer it.

I'm very hot! (open a window)
I'll open a window.

We haven't got any milk! (go to the shop)
I'll go to the shop.

Unit 6 Step 1

First conditional

Listen to the example, then say what Sarah will and won't do.

If I don't pass my exam, I won't be happy.
If she doesn't pass her exam, she won't be happy.

If it rains tomorrow, I'll stay at home.
If it rains tomorrow, she'll stay at home.

If I see Laura, I'll tell her.
If she sees Laura, she'll tell her.

If I eat too much, I'll be ill.
If she eats too much, she'll be ill.

If I don't ring John, he'll be worried.
If she doesn't ring John, he'll be worried.

If it's sunny tomorrow, I'll play tennis.
If it's sunny tomorrow, she'll play tennis.

Unit 6 Step 1

Could I / Could you . . . ?

Listen to the example, then make polite requests with *Could I . . . ?* or *Could you . . . ?*

I want to use the phone.
Could I use the phone, please?

I'd like to go with you.
Could I go with you, please?

I want to talk to you.
Could I talk to you, please?

I'd like to look at the menu.
Could I look at the menu, please?

Close the door.
Could you close the door, please?

Pass me the salt.
Could you pass me the salt, please?

Unit 7 Step 1

Present perfect: questions and short answers

Listen to the example, then answer the questions.

Have you painted your room? (yes)
Yes, I have.

Has your sister changed her hair? (no)
No, she hasn't.

Has Sam used his new bike? (yes)
Yes, he has.

Have Tim and Penny built some shelves? (yes)
Yes, they have.

Have you bought some new shoes? (yes)
Yes, I have.

Unit 7 Step 1  Class CD 2 Track 4

2 Present perfect: questions

What have these people done? Listen to the example, then make questions.

Sarah's done her homework. (tidied her room)
Has she tidied her room?

I've eaten all my carrots. (eaten all your potatoes)
Have you eaten all your potatoes?

David has made his bed. (had a shower)
Has he had a shower?

We've bought some eggs. (bought any bread)
Have you bought any bread?

Unit 8 Step 1  Class CD 2 Track 12

Present perfect + *just*

Listen to the example, then answer the questions.

Has Sam washed the car?
Yes, he's just washed it.

Have your parents arrived?
Yes, they've just arrived.

Has the film started?
Yes, it's just started.

Has Clara phoned?
Yes, she's just phoned.

Have you eaten?
Yes, I've just eaten.

Unit 8 Step 2  Class CD 2 Track 14

How long . . . ?

Listen to the example, then make questions with *How long . . . ?*

I've got a motorbike.
How long have you had it?

John lives in New York now.
How long has he lived there?

David and Carl are in a pop group.
How long have they been in a pop group?

Christina wears glasses.
How long has she worn glasses?

Unit 9 Step 1  Class CD 2 Track 21

1 *have to*

Listen to the example, then make sentences.

Laura / wear a school uniform
Laura has to wear a school uniform.

Michael and Maria / work on Saturday.
Michael and Maria have to work on Saturday.

Sarah / go to bed at ten o'clock.
Sarah has to go to bed at ten o'clock.

I / walk to school.
I have to walk to school.

Ana's friends / a lot of exams
Ana's friends have to do a lot of exams.

PATTERN DRILLS

Unit 9 Step 1  Class CD 2 Track 22

 don't have to

 Today is Monday, but it's a holiday. Listen to the example, then say why today is different for these people.

Mel normally has to work, but today
she doesn't have to work.

I normally have to go to school, but today
I don't have to go to school.

Edward normally has to get the train, but today
he doesn't have to get the train.

We normally have to make a packed lunch, but today
we don't have to make a packed lunch.

Unit 9 Step 2  Class CD 2 Track 26

should / shouldn't

Listen to the example, then give advice.

I've got a headache. (take an aspirin)
You should take an aspirin.

I'm not very healthy. (not smoke)
You shouldn't smoke.

I'm tired. (go to bed)
You should go to bed.

I've got an important exam tomorrow. (do some revision)
You should do some revision.

I've got a cold. (not go out)
You shouldn't go out.

Unit 10 Step 2  Class CD 2 Track 33

Past simple passive: affirmative

Listen to the example, then answer the questions.

Who was *Yesterday* sung by? (The Beatles)
It was sung by The Beatles.

When was John Lennon killed? (1980)
He was killed in 1980.

Who were the Harry Potter books written by? (J.K. Rowling)
They were written by J.K. Rowling.

Where was the Mona Lisa painted? (Italy)
It was painted in Italy.

When was the Eiffel Tower built? (1889)
It was built in 1889.

Unit 11 Step 1  Class CD 2 Track 42

Reported speech: affirmative

Listen to the example, then make sentences.

My name's Edward.
He said his name was Edward.

I'm from England.
He said he was from England.

I go to Westfield school.
He said he went to Westfield school.

I speak three languages.
He said he spoke three languages.

I've got a sister.
He said he had a sister.

Unit 11 Step 2  Class CD 2 Track 45

Question tags

 Listen to the examples, then make questions using question tags.

You're English.
You're English, aren't you?

You live in London.
You live in London, don't you?

You can't swim.
You can't swim, can you?

You don't like school.
You don't like school, do you?

You've got a cold.
You've got a cold, haven't you?

Unit 12 Step 1 Class CD 2 Track 51

used to

Listen to the example, then make sentences with *used to*.

I smoked before, but I don't smoke now.
I used to smoke.

Helen lived in New York, but she doesn't live there now.
She used to live in New York.

I had long hair last year, but now it's short.
I used to have long hair.

My dad was a teacher, but now he's a writer.
He used to be a teacher.

I had a hamster, but it died.
I used to have a hamster.

Unit 12 Step 2  Class CD 2 Track 54

Second conditional

Listen to the example, then complete the sentences using the second conditional.

If I won the lottery (buy / big house)
I'd buy a big house.

If Laura could swim (go / swimming pool)
she'd go to the swimming pool.

If Paul and Maria had a car (drive to work)
they'd drive to work.

If Sam was older (learn to drive)
he'd learn to drive.

If I didn't have to go to school (watch TV all day)
I'd watch TV all day.

PATTERN DRILLS

Unit 1

Grammar practice key

1 2 d 3 h 4 e 5 b 6 g 7 a 8 c

2 2 Yes, I have 3 No, she doesn't 4 Yes, they are 5 No, I'm not 6 No, he isn't 7 Yes, they do 8 No, she hasn't

3 2 Is – Does 3 are – do 4 Have – Has 5 Is – Are 6 do – are 7 Are – Have 8 Are – Do

4 2 's talking 3 's wearing 4 go 5 don't speak 6 're watching 7 isn't raining / is not raining 8 has

Communication activity

● For further practice of questions and answers, use the information gap activity on page 24. Make photocopies of the page and cut them into A and B sheets for each pair in the class.

● To prepare students for the activity, ask a few questions. For example: *Are you French? Do you live in London? Can you swim?* etc. to elicit short answers and then get the students to do the same with you.

● Students imagine they are the boy described in their sheets and read the information about themselves. Both students then work together to complete the true/false exercise.

● Stronger classes could do the activity without referring to the original text.

Answers

Student A: 1 T 2 F 3 F 4 F 5 T 6 T 7 T 8 F 9 T 10 F

Student B: 1 F 2 F 3 F 4 T 5 T 6 F 7 T 8 F 9 T 10 F

Unit 2

Grammar practice key

1 2 did you get to, f
3 were you, h
4 did Paul have, d
5 did you do, a
6 was your brother, e
7 did Carla get up, b
8 did you give, g

2 2 didn't sing 3 saw 4 didn't go out 5 got 6 sent

3 2 e 3 a 4 g 5 h 6 c 7 b 8 f

4 2 were singing
3 was listening
4 were having
5 was playing
6 was raining

Communication activity

● For further practice of the past continuous, use the memory game on page 26. Make photocopies of the page and cut them into A and B sheets for each pair in the class. Make sure they cannot see each other's pictures.

● Tell students that they are looking at a situation at 4.30 yesterday afternoon and elicit that we use the past continuous to describe the actions of the different people in the picture.

● Give the students 10 minutes to write at least five questions (in the past continuous) about the scene.

● Students swap their pictures and have a maximum of two minutes to study their new picture. When the time is up, they swap back their pictures.

● Students ask each other five of their questions. They should try to respond with complete sentences using the past continuous. They should keep a score of their correct answers. Act as referee in cases of doubt.

● For weaker groups it might be an idea to have the students work in pairs (i.e. two student As) to prepare their questions before linking up with a new partner for the question and answer session.

Unit 3

Grammar practice key

1 2 more independent than 3 the most popular 4 the laziest 5 faster than 6 hotter than 7 best 8 curlier than

2 2 wasn't as good as 3 isn't as old as 4 isn't as big as 5 isn't as long as 6 isn't as expensive as 7 aren't as fast as 8 isn't as easy as

3 2 is 3 Are 4 Do 5 are 6 does 7 is 8 do 2 g 3 b 4 f 5 h 6 e 7 c 8 a

4 2 old 3 funnier 4 worst 5 from 6 most 7 as 8 more expensive

Communication activity

● For further practice of comparatives and superlatives, use the 'spot the difference' activity on page 28. Make photocopies of the page and cut them into A and B sheets for each pair in the class. Make sure they cannot see each other's pictures.

- Students take it in turns to describe the people in their picture and find six differences between their pictures. Encourage them to use comparatives and superlatives as in the given examples.

Unit 4

Grammar practice key

1 2 Let's – c   3 going – a   4 Shall – f   5 visiting – g   6 go – d   7 Shall – b   8 visit – h

2 2 too much   3 too much   4 too many
5 too much   6 too much

3 2 are too many
3 buys too many / spends too much (money) on
4 haven't got enough
5 is too much

4 2 a lot of   3 many   4 much
5 enough   6 a lot of

Communication activity

- For further practice of making and responding to suggestions, use the activity on page 30. Students need to work in pairs. Make photocopies of the page and give one copy to each pair of students. You will also need a coin and scissors for each pair.
- Using a coin, demonstrate meaning of 'toss a coin' and 'heads' and 'tails'.
- Explain to students that they are on holiday in Sydney, Australia with a friend. They are trying to decide what they can do and where they can go.
- Before beginning the activity, recap the different structures used in the unit.
- Students cut out the cards and place them in a pile, facing down. (Alternatively, you can cut out one set of cards for each pair before the class.)
- Student A, using the information on the card, must make a suggestion (*Shall we go swimming on Thursday afternoon?*).
- Student B must toss the coin. If the coin lands 'heads' up, he/she must accept the offer (*Yes, that's a good idea!*). If the coin lands 'tails' up, Student B must apologise politely and give a reason (*I'm sorry, I can't. I'm going to the cinema.*).
- Student B then continues by picking a new card and making a suggestion. This time, Student A must toss the coin and answer.
- Students continue to take turns until all the cards have been used.

Unit 5

Grammar practice key

1 2 g   3 f   4 h   5 e   6 b   7 a   8 c

2 2 's working   6 are we going to do
3 'm not doing   7 's going to have
4 Is your dad meeting   8 isn't going to buy

3 2 'll   3 won't   4 'll   5 'll   6 won't

4 2 are you going to paint
3 is going to get
4 'll go
5 's going to stop
6 will/'ll babysit

Communication activity

- For further practice of the present continuous for arrangements, use the information gap activity on page 32. Make photocopies of the page and cut them into A and B sheets for each pair in the class. Make sure they cannot see each other's sheets.
- Students take it in turns to ask about Sarah's arrangements and to complete the table. When they finish, they should compare their sheets to ensure they have completed the information correctly.

Unit 6

Grammar practice key

1 2 are ... 'll visit
3 won't win ... lose
4 'll play ... doesn't rain
5 goes ... 'll learn
6 eat ... won't be able to
7 will be ... don't do
8 won't be able to ... isn't better

2 2 Could you help me with this exercise? – f
3 What would you like? – a
4 Can I stay at Jane's house on Friday night? – h
5 I'd like the chocolate mousse for dessert, please. – g
6 Could you close the door, please? – e
7 I'd like a new computer for Christmas. – d
8 Could you pass me the water, please? – b

3 2 will / 'll   3 might ... might   4 will / 'll
5 won't   6 might not   7 will / 'll
8 won't / might not

4   2   might not – won't
3   Do – Can/Could
4   will – might
5   Will – Can/Could
6   might – will

Communication activity

- For further practice of making predictions about the future, use the activity on page 34. Make photocopies of the page and cut them into A and B sheets for each pair in the class.

- Give students five or ten minutes to think about their predictions before beginning the activity. They could make notes, but they should not write complete sentences at this stage.

- Students then exchange their predictions. Encourage them to ask questions using *Will I . . . ?*

- When they finish, they could change partners and report to their new partners what they have just been told about their futures (for example, *I will live in Brazil*).

- Before beginning the activity, it might be an idea to give some examples by giving your own invented predictions to a few students. This should encourage them to use a variety of different structures rather than the basic *You will . . .*

Unit 7

Grammar practice key

1   2   bought – they haven't
3   eaten – I haven't
4   made – I have
5   cut – he has
6   stopped – it hasn't
7   passed – she has
8   learnt – I haven't

2   2 has written   3 haven't turned off   4 has read
5 have made   6 haven't eaten   7 hasn't done
8 have brought

3   2   Have Annie and Ian changed their phone number?
3   Has your sister found her rucksack?
4   Have you and Lillian met my cousin?
5   Has it stopped raining?
6   Have you heard the new Eminem album?
7   Has Jack bought a PlayStation?
8   Has Ellie invited Tania to the barbecue?

4   2 Did you see   3 went   4 have lost   5 hasn't eaten   6 saw   7 have got   8 Have you finished

Communication activity

- For further practice of the present perfect for finished actions, use the information gap activity on page 36. Make photocopies of the page and cut them into A and B sheets for each pair in the class. Make sure they cannot see each other's sheets.

- Students take it in turns to ask if Kerry and Christine have done the jobs on their lists. When they are asked, the students should check by looking at the picture and answering appropriately. Items on the list should then be ticked or crossed accordingly.

Unit 8

Grammar practice key

1   2   Holland has never won the World Cup.
3   Barry has just seen a snake!
4   What has Tom just done?
5   My grandfather has never been abroad.
6   Have you ever met a famous person?
7   I have never been to China.
8   I have just spoken to Steve.

2   2   for
3   since
4   since
5   for
6   for
7   since
8   for

3   2   Jack's mum and dad have been married since 1991.
3   I've known you for seven years.
4   I've liked U2 since 1998.
5   Kevin has lived in Birmingham since he was four.
6   My sister has been a nurse for ten months.

4   2   How long have Jack's mum and dad been married?
3   How long have you known me?
4   How long have you liked U2?
5   How long has Kevin lived in Birmingham?
6   How long has your sister been a nurse?

Communication activity

- For further practice of the present perfect for achievements and periods of time, use the information gap activity on page 38. Make photocopies of the page and cut them into A and B sheets for each pair in the class. Make sure they cannot see each other's sheets.

- Students read the information about their character. They take it in turns to ask questions to find if their sentences are true or false. Stronger classes could do the activity without referring to the original text.

Answers

Student A: 1 T 2 F 3 F 4 T 5 T 6 F 7 T 8 F 9 F 10 F

Student B: 1 F 2 F 3 F 4 T 5 F 6 T 7 F 8 F 9 F 10 T

Unit 9

Grammar practice key

1
2 has to 3 don't have to 4 have to
5 don't have to 6 has to 7 have to
8 doesn't have to

2
2 don't have to 3 doesn't have to 4 mustn't
5 mustn't 6 don't have to 7 mustn't
8 don't have to

3
2 shouldn't go out with
3 should look for
4 should go
5 should take
6 shouldn't spend

4
2 c 3 c 4 a 5 c 6 b

Communication activity

- For further practice of words for the body, illnesses and injuries, use the crossword on page 40. Make photocopies of the page and cut them into A and B sheets for each pair in the class. Make sure they cannot see each other's sheets.

- Students look at their crosswords and decide how they are going to describe the words in their crossword to their partner.

- Students take it in turns to ask about a missing word in their crossword. They should help each other with spelling if necessary.

Unit 10

Grammar practice key

1
2 e 3 b 4 a 5 d 6 f

2
2 is spoken 3 are bought
4 is served 5 is produced

3
2 were made 3 were built
4 were held 5 was invented

4
2 When were these houses built? – were built
3 Which languages are taught at this school? – are taught
4 Who was *Hamlet* written by? – was written
5 Where was John Lennon killed? – was killed
6 Where are bananas grown? – are grown

Communication activity

- For further practice of past simple passive and revision of information in Unit 10, use the board game on page 42. Photocopy the page for each group of four players. Each group will also need a dice and counters.

- Students work in teams of two. One person rolls the dice. If the team lands on a question square, one player forms the question in the passive and the other has to answer it with a complete sentence. If they are correct, they stay on the square and play passes to the other team. If they answer incorrectly, they move back three squares. If there are any doubts over answers or grammatical forms, you should act as referee. If a team lands on any of the other squares, they should follow the instructions. Students in each team should take it in turns to ask and answer questions.

- The first team to finish is the winner.

- If you feel the class will not remember much of the information from the unit, you could give the students a few minutes before beginning to look through the unit.

Answers

1 1939 2 *Spacewar* 3 George Lucas
4 Chicago 5 1853 6 Mickey Mouse 7 Picasso
8 1889 9 John F. Kennedy 10 Judy Garland
11 1937 12 Athens 13 Italy 14 Van Gogh
15 1962 16 1995 17 France

Unit 11

Grammar practice key

1
2 say 3 tells 4 said 5 said 6 told 7 tell
8 said

2
2 said – told
3 told – said
4 were – was
5 got – had
6 we – they

3
  2 Benny said he had a lot of homework.

  3 John told Maria he couldn't find his keys.

  4 Tina said she wasn't the tallest person in her class.

  5 Jim and Dawn said they left home at 7.30 every morning.

  6 Fiona said she didn't argue with her sister.

  7 Patrick said his mum and dad were at the supermarket.

  8 Karen told me she loved me.

4
  2 is 3 can't 4 don't 5 were 6 isn't 7 did
  8 won't 9 are 10 was

Communication activity

- For further practice of reported speech, use the information gap activity on page 44. Make photocopies of the page and cut them into A and B sheets for each pair in the class. Make sure they cannot see each other's sheets.

- Students look at their pictures and take it in turns to ask their partners about the empty speech bubbles. They fill in the bubbles with direct speech. When they answer a question they should use reported speech.

- Students compare pictures when they have finished and check for possible mistakes.

Unit 12

Grammar practice key

1
  2 used to live

  3 used to smoke

  4 didn't use to be

  5 didn't use to be

  6 didn't use to wear

2
  2 went, it would

  3 used, she wouldn't

  4 lived, you would

  5 played, he would

  6 caught, it wouldn't

  7 were, I would

  8 gave, I would

3
  2 met ... would be

  3 studied ... wouldn't need

  4 wasn't ... would like

  5 didn't cut ... would be

  6 helped ... would finish

4
  2 lived in the USA I'd play

  3 wasn't (so) hot, I'd drink

  4 did (some) exercise, you wouldn't be

  5 could speak Portuguese, I'd go

Communication activity

- For further practice of the second conditional, use the activity on page 46. Photocopy the page for each pair or small group.

- Students first use the cues to create a second conditional sentence to describe the person in each picture. For example, *If Paul was invisible, he wouldn't pay to go to the cinema.*

- They then take it in turns to ask and answer questions, using the second conditional.

- At the end, there could be class feedback of what different students would do in the different situations shown in the pictures.

- Before starting the activity, It might be a good idea to use the first picture (Paul) as an example with the class. With weaker classes, you could elicit the sentences for each picture.

1 Questions and answers

Match the questions in A with the answers in B.

A

1 Have you got a bike?

2 Does Ben like football?

3 Are you going to the supermarket?

4 What do you do in the evening?

5 Are you cold?

6 Do you get up early on Monday morning?

7 What are you doing?

8 Why are you running?

B

a I'm reading a magazine.

b No, I'm not. I'm hot.

c Because I'm late.

d Yes, he does.

e I usually do my homework.

f ~~Yes, I have.~~

g Yes, I do.

h No, I'm going to the station.

1 _f_   2 _____   3 _____   4 _____   5 _____   6 _____   7 _____   8 _____

2 Short answers

Complete the answers to these questions.

1 Are you all right?   Yes, _I am_ .

2 Have you got a CD player?   Yes, _____ .

3 Does your mother like burgers? No, _____ .

4 Are Mel and Laura your sisters? Yes, _____ .

5 Are you going to the park?   No, _____ .

6 Is your brother at home?   No, _____ .

7 Do Anna's parents come
   from Poland?   Yes, _____ .

8 Has Victoria got any pets?   No, _____ .

3 Questions

Look for a mistake in each question. Underline the mistake and correct it.

1 <u>Are</u> your name John?   _Is_

2 Is Jane have cereal for breakfast? _____

3 Where are you live?   _____

4 Have your brother got a computer?   _____

5 Is you homesick?   _____

6 What do you doing at the moment?   _____

7 Are Tom and Sarah got a new TV?   _____

8 Are your cousins usually go to
   the country at the weekend?   _____

4 Present simple and present continuous

Complete the sentences with the present simple or the present continuous.

1 Bernie usually _plays_ (play)
   basketball at the weekend.

2 Julie _____ (talk) to Dad at
   the moment.

3 Look, there's Tim! He _____
   (wear) new glasses!

4 We _____ (go) to the beach
   every summer.

5 My parents are from Greece but I
   _____ (not speak) Greek.

6 Alan and Sam are at the cinema. They
   _____ (watch) the new Tom
   Cruise film.

7 Great, we can play tennis because it
   _____ (not rain).

8 My uncle sometimes _____
   (have) a cup of coffee after lunch.

Student A

1 Imagine you are Paul. Read the information about yourself and then answer your partner's questions. Your partner's name is Pablo.

B: Are you German?   A: No, I'm not.

> Your name is Paul and you come from Lyon in France. You're 14 years old and you're studying English in Manchester. You like England, but you're a bit homesick because your parents and younger brother are in Lyon. Your mother's name is Marie and she's a painter. Your father, Roberto, is from Italy and he's a pilot. You like swimming and tennis. You also like music and films. You've got all Eminem's CDs and you love watching horror films. You don't like studying and you think reading is boring. At the moment, you're writing an email to your brother.

2 Work with your partner. Ask questions to find out if the following sentences are true or false.

A: Are you 16?

1	Pablo is 16 years old.	6	His mother works in a hospital.
2	His favourite school subject is maths.	7	He's studying English.
3	He comes from Mexico.	8	He speaks German.
4	He hasn't got a sister.	9	He can play the guitar.
5	His father is a doctor.	10	At the moment, he's listening to music.

Student B

1 Your partner's name is Paul. Ask questions to find out if the following sentences are true or false.

B: Are you German?

1	Paul comes from Germany.	6	He's 15 years old.
2	He hasn't got any brothers or sisters.	7	His father is from Italy.
3	He likes reading horror books.	8	At the moment, he's living in London.
4	His favourite singer is Eminem.	9	He's homesick.
5	At the moment, he's writing an email.	10	He can't swim.

2 Imagine you are Pablo. Read the information about yourself and then answer your partner's questions.

A: Are you 16?   B: Yes, I am.

> Your name is Pablo and you come from Malaga in Spain. You're 16 years old and at the moment you're staying with your uncle in London to practise your English. You love London and British music. You play the guitar in a band in Madrid. Your mother, Carmen, is a doctor and she works in the same hospital as your father, Carlos, who is a nurse. You're a good student and you really like science. You know that English is a useful language. You also speak some French and Italian. At the moment, you're shopping. You want to buy a present for your sister, Patricia.

Messages 3 PHOTOCOPIABLE © Cambridge University Press 2006 Module 1 resources Unit 1

1 Past simple: *Wh-* questions

Complete the questions using the past simple. Then match them with the answers (a–h).

1 Where ___did they go___ (they / go) for their holiday?
2 How _____ (you / get to) Kate's house last night?
3 Where _____ (you / be) yesterday?
4 When _____ (Paul / have) his party?
5 What _____ (you / do) after the film?
6 Why _____ (your brother / be) late for school?
7 What time _____ (Carla / get up) yesterday?
8 What _____ (you / give) your dad for his birthday?

a We went to Pizza Express.
b At 11.30!
c ~~They went to France.~~
d Last Saturday.
e He didn't hear his alarm clock.
f We caught the bus.
g I gave him a watch.
h I was at home all day.

1 __c__ 2 _____ 3 _____ 4 _____ 5 _____ 6 _____ 7 _____ 8 _____

2 Past simple: affirmative and negative

Use the past simple form of the verbs in the box to make sentences.

| get   not sing   ~~not be~~   see   go out   send |

1 We lost 5–1. We ___weren't___ very good.
2 Elvis Presley _____ in Greek!
3 I _____ David Beckham yesterday!
4 I _____ last night. I was very tired.
5 Teresa _____ a taxi to the theatre because she didn't want to walk.
6 I _____ you a text message yesterday. Did you get it?

3 Past simple and past continuous

Match the words in A with the words in B and make sentences.

A
1 I learnt French when
2 When James arrived home
3 Peter and Ana were walking in the park when
4 The students were running around the classroom when
5 I was standing outside the cinema when
6 When Amelia looked out of the window
7 Tina was tidying the living room when
8 My dad was studying history at university when

B
a they saw Tommy.
b she broke the lamp.
c she saw that it was snowing.
d ~~I was living in Paris.~~
e his parents were having lunch.
f he met my mum.
g the teacher came in.
h I saw the accident.

1 __d__ 2 _____ 3 _____ 4 _____ 5 _____ 6 _____ 7 _____ 8 _____

4 Past continuous: affirmative

Use the past continuous form of the verbs in the box to make sentences.

| rain   play   ~~talk~~   leave   have   sing   walk   listen |

1 I ___was talking___ on the phone when I heard the explosion.
2 When Annie woke up, the birds _____ .
3 Dad _____ to the radio when we arrived.
4 The phone rang when we _____ lunch.
5 Tom _____ football when he broke his leg.
6 It _____ when we got to the beach.

Student A

1 Look at this picture of what was happening at 4.30 yesterday afternoon. Your teacher will give you *ten minutes* to write at least five questions about the scene in the **past continuous**:

What was Fiona eating? Was Carol reading a book or a magazine?

2 Swap your picture with your partner, who will give you a different picture to look at. You have *two minutes* to study this picture and remember what was happening.

3 Swap back your pictures. Ask your partner five of the questions you wrote in 1. Your partner will ask you five questions about their picture. The person who answers the most questions correctly is the winner!

Student B

1 Look at this picture of what was happening at 4.30 yesterday afternoon. Your teacher will give you *ten minutes* to write at least five questions about the scene in the **past continuous**:

What was Frank buying? Was Edward drinking water or coke?

2 Swap your picture with your partner who will give you a different picture to look at. You have *two minutes* to study this picture and remember what was happening.

3 Swap back your pictures. Ask your partner five of the questions you wrote in 1. Your partner will ask you five questions about their picture. The person who answers the most questions correctly is the winner!

1 Comparatives and superlatives

Make sentences with the comparative or superlative form of the adjectives in brackets.

1 Bill Gates is ___the richest___ man in the world. (rich)

2 Cats are _____ dogs. (independent)

3 Table tennis is _____ sport in China. (popular)

4 John is _____ boy in the class. He never does any work! (lazy)

5 Cheetahs can run _____ _____ horses. (fast)

6 Morocco is _____ Sweden. (hot)

7 My _____ friend's name is Paul. (good)

8 Julie's hair is _____ Sally's. (curly)

2 as ... as

Complete the sentences. Use *as ... as*.

1 Kerry is 1.73 metres tall and Angela is 1.62 metres tall.
Angela ___isn't as tall as___ Kerry.

2 The book was better than the film.
The film _____ the book.

3 Simon is 15 years old and David is 14.
David _____ Simon.

4 China is the biggest country in the world.
England _____ China.

5 Claire has got longer hair than Jane.
Jane's hair _____ Claire's.

6 The DVD costs £11.99 and the book costs £6.99.
The book _____ the DVD.

7 Bikes are slower than cars.
Bikes _____ cars.

8 Maths is more difficult than English.
Maths _____ English.

3 Asking for a description

Complete the questions using the words in the box. Then match the questions with the answers (a–h).

| do (x2)   does   is (x3)   are (x2) |

1 What ___is___ Tom like?

2 What _____ your school like?

3 _____ you as lazy as your brother?

4 _____ you look like your brother?

5 What _____ your grandparents like?

6 What _____ Tom look like?

7 What _____ your flat like?

8 What _____ you look like?

a I've got short black hair and I wear glasses.

b No, I'm more hard-working than him.

c It's nice. It's got three bedrooms and a big living room.

d ~~He's very generous and quite clever.~~

e He's quite tall. He's got blue eyes and he's very good-looking.

f No, he's much taller than me and he's got darker hair.

g It's very big. It's got more than 2000 students.

h They're quite easy-going.

1 ___d___   2 _____   3 _____   4 _____
5 _____   6 _____   7 _____   8 _____

4 Comparatives and superlatives

Underline the right words.

1 My brothers are *tallers / taller* than my father.

2 Anne isn't as *older / old* as Toby.

3 Louise is *funnier / more funny* than Elizabeth.

4 I think it's the *baddest / worst* song in the world!

5 Indian food is very different *of / from* Italian food.

6 Jane is the *most / more* intelligent girl in the class.

7 American football isn't the same *as / that* soccer.

8 The theatre is *more expensive / expensiver* than the cinema.

RESOURCES UNIT 3   GRAMMAR PRACTICE

Student A

Describe Sarah, Jane and Angela.

Listen to your partner describe Sarah, Jane and Angela. Find six differences between your pictures and your partner's pictures.

A: Sarah's hair isn't as long as Angela's hair.   B: In my picture Angela's hair is shorter than Sarah's hair.

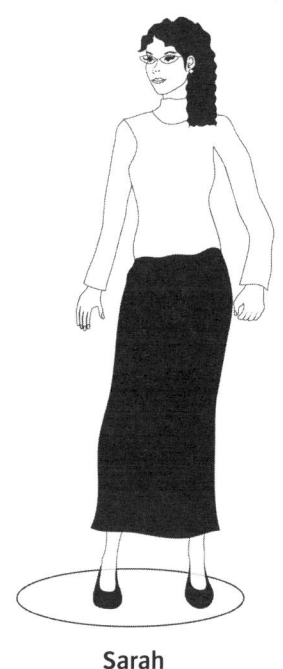

Sarah

Jane

Angela

Student B

Describe Sarah, Jane and Angela.

Listen to your partner describe Sarah, Jane and Angela. Find six differences between your pictures and your partner's pictures.

B: Jane's the tallest.   A: In my picture Sarah's the tallest.

Jane

Angela

Sarah

1 Suggestions

Complete these suggestions using the words in the box. Then match the suggestions with the responses (a–h).

go	shall (x3)	going	visit	let's	visiting

1 _Shall_ we go and see the match tomorrow?

2 _____ have a picnic tomorrow.

3 How about _____ to that new department store?

4 _____ we meet at the art gallery?

5 How about _____ my grandad after school?

6 Why don't we _____ shopping tomorrow?

7 _____ we leave early?

8 Let's _____ the Royal Palace.

a All right then. They've got some good sports clothes.

b That's fine with me. How about 7.30?

c That's a nice idea, but I think it's going to rain.

d I don't mind, but I haven't got much money.

e OK, but I hope we can get tickets.

f I'd rather meet outside the mosque. It's nearer.

g Are you sure he'll be at home?

h Oh no! Kings and queens . . . it's really boring!

1	_e_	2	___	3	___	4	___
5	___	6	___	7	___	8	___

2 too much / many

Complete the sentences with *too much* or *too many*.

1 There are _too many_ students in my class!

2 There's _____ snow! We can't play football today.

3 I've got _____ homework.

4 Greg has got bad teeth because he eats _____ sweets.

5 I prefer the country – there's _____ pollution in the city.

6 This soup has got _____ salt in it.

3 too much / many, not enough

Rewrite the sentences. Use *too much, too many* or *not enough*.

1 Zoe wants to finish her homework, but she needs more information.
Zoe _hasn't got enough_ information to finish her homework.

2 There are 14 boys who want to play, but we only need 11.
There _____ boys for the team.

3 Liam's mum is fed up because he spends all his money on video games.
Liam's mum thinks he _____ _____ video games.

4 There are a lot of people at the party, but there isn't much food.
We _____ food for everyone.

5 The library is very noisy and I can't concentrate.
I can't concentrate because there _____ _____ noise.

4 much, many, a lot of or enough

Complete the sentences. Use *much, many, a lot of* or *enough*.

1 Have you got _many_ brothers and sisters?

2 I love Paris! I went to _____ interesting museums and art galleries when I was there.

3 We didn't see _____ bands at the festival because we got there late.

4 People in Spain don't drink _____ tea. They prefer coffee.

5 Have you got _____ meat or would you like another piece?

6 I bought _____ CDs on Saturday.

go swimming / Thursday afternoon?	have a picnic / weekend?
play tennis / Saturday morning?	look round the shops / tomorrow?
have lunch at a restaurant / Friday evening?	see the new Penelope Cruz film / after dinner?
have a barbecue / Sunday afternoon?	go to Sydney Football Stadium / Saturday afternoon?
visit the Sydney Art Gallery / Tuesday morning?	take a boat trip / tonight?
go to the Wonderland theme park / Sunday?	visit the mosque / Thursday morning?
look round a department store / Wednesday afternoon?	visit Sydney Opera House / Monday morning?
go to the threatre / Tuesday evening?	watch a DVD / tomorrow?
visit Tarongo zoo / next Wednesday?	visit the Koala Park / Thursday?
go to the Aquarium / Monday afternoon?	look round the Australian Museum / Friday morning?

1 The future: all forms

Match the sentences in A with the sentences in B.

A

1 It's hot in here.

2 Robbie Williams is coming! I think I'll go and see him!

3 What are you going to do at the weekend?

4 I'm going to see Jamelia next week.

5 Are you busy tomorrow?

6 I think I'll stay at home tonight.

7 Hang on. I must get something from my bedroom.

8 I like this skirt.

B

a I won't be a minute.

b I'm fed up of going out every night.

c I'll try it on.

d I'll open a window.

e Yes, I'm meeting Lucy and Chris for lunch at 1.30.

f I'm going to stay in bed. I'm exhausted!

g I'll get my ticket tomorrow.

h They say she's really good in concert.

1 _d_   2 _____   3 _____   4 _____   5 _____   6 _____   7 _____   8 _____

2 The future with the present continuous and *going to*

Complete these sentences. Use the present continuous for future arrangements and *going to* for intentions.

Future arrangements:

1 What time _are you seeing_ (you / see) Steve this evening?

2 Vicky can't come. She _____ (work) tomorrow night.

3 No, I'm not busy tonight. I _____ _____ (not do) anything.

4 _____ (your dad / meet) you after school?

Intentions:

5 We _'re going to visit_ (visit) Andrew in hospital. Do you want to come?

6 I can't find my key. What _____ (we / do)?

7 Luke's brother _____ (have) a party for his 16th birthday!

8 Sue _____ (not buy) the white boots. They're too expensive.

3 will/won't

Complete the sentences. Use *will* ('*ll*) or *won't*.

1 There isn't any bread. I _'ll_ go to the baker's.

2 Oh look! They've got pizza. I _____ have that.

3 I _____ go to the party. I don't feel well.

4 I _____ help you with your homework.

5 I'm not sure which I prefer. I think I _____ get the blue one.

6 I _____ see you tomorrow because I'm going to help my aunt at her shop.

4 will or going to?

Complete the sentences. Use *will* ('*ll*) or *going to*.

1 Is it 4.30 already? OK, we _'ll_ finish this tomorrow.

2 Why _____ (you paint) your bedroom? I like the colour you've got now.

3 Alice is _____ (get) a job in the summer because she wants to buy a car.

4 I'm going into town so I _____ (go) to the supermarket for you.

5 Hannah says she _____ (stop) eating fast food because it's not very healthy.

6 Don't worry! Jenny says that she _____ (babysit) for you.

Student A

Here is a list of Sarah's arrangements for next week. Some of the information is missing. Take it in turns to ask and answer questions. Complete the table.

A: What's Sarah doing on Monday?

	what?	where?	what time?
Monday	....	school	....
Tuesday	piano lesson	Mr Briggs' house	6.20
Wednesday	tennis	park	7.00
Thursday	visit Philip	hospital	....
Friday	shopping	....	5.00
Friday	disco	Zeppelin	8.00
Saturday	tennis	....	....
Saturday	....	....	9.00
Sunday	lunch	Grandad's house	2.15
Sunday	babysitting	the Evans' house	6.30

Student B

Here is a list of Sarah's arrangements for next week. Some of the information is missing. Take it in turns to ask and answer questions. Complete the table.

B: What's Sarah doing on Tuesday?

	what?	where?	what time?
Monday	maths exam	school	11.00
Tuesday	....	Mr Briggs' house	6.20
Wednesday	tennis	....	....
Thursday	visit Philip	hospital	7.15
Friday	shopping	Arndale Centre	5.00
Friday	....	Zeppelin	....
Saturday	tennis	park	1.00
Saturday	party	Jane's house	9.00
Sunday	....	....	2.15
Sunday	babysitting	the Evans' house	....

1 First conditional

Complete the sentences.

1 If I _don't see_ (not see) you tomorrow, I'll see (see) you at the weekend.

2 If enough people _____ (be) interested, we _____ (visit) the Science Museum.

3 Arsenal _____ (not win) the championship if they _____ (lose) the next two matches.

4 I _____ (play) tennis with you tomorrow if it _____ (not rain).

5 If José _____ (go) to Britain in the summer, he _____ (learn) a lot of English.

6 If you _____ (eat) too many chips, you _____ (not be able to) eat a dessert.

7 The teacher _____ (be) annoyed if you _____ (not do) your homework.

8 Sadie _____ (not be able to) play if her leg _____ (not be better) soon.

2 Polite requests

Put the words in the right order and make sentences. Then match the sentences to the responses (a–h).

1 I / can / phone / use / your
Can I use your phone ?

2 help / could / me / exercise / with / you / this
_____ ?

3 you / like / would / what
_____ ?

4 Jane's / can / stay / on / night / house / I / at / Friday
_____ ?

5 the / please / like / for / chocolate mousse / I'd / dessert
_____ .

6 please / you / could / door / the / close
_____ ?

7 computer / for / new / like / a / Christmas / I'd
_____ .

8 water / pass / you / please / me / could / the
_____ ?

a I think I'll have the soup, please.

b Sure. Have you got a glass?

c Of course! It's in the hall.

d They're very expensive, you know.

e Why? Are you cold?

f I'll try, but I don't really understand it myself.

g Mmm, that's my favourite, too.

h Are you sure her parents say it's OK?

1 _c_   2 ____   3 ____   4 ____   5 ____

6 ____   7 ____   8 ____

3 will and might

Complete the sentences with will ('ll), won't, might or might not.

1 We ____'ll____ probably go to Disneyland if we go to the USA.

2 I promise I _____ write to you.

3 Tracey says she _____ meet us at the restaurant, or she _____ come to our house first.

4 I've got the best friends in the world. I _____ really miss them if I go to live in Canada.

5 Penny's got a terrible memory. She probably _____ remember your birthday.

6 I _____ be able to go on Sunday. I don't know if I've got enough money. I'll tell you tomorrow.

7 I _____ have the fish, please.

8 Michael _____ eat the lasagne. He doesn't like pasta.

4 Can/could, will and might

Look for a mistake in each sentence. Underline the mistake and correct it.

1 I'll like the salad for a starter, please. _I'd_

2 Dan probably might not pass the exam.
_____

3 Do you tell me the time, please?
_____

4 I'm not sure, but I will have chicken for lunch.
_____

5 Will I watch the basketball, please?
_____

6 I promise I might always love you!
_____

Student A

1 Look at the pictures and write predictions about your partner's future. Use your imagination!

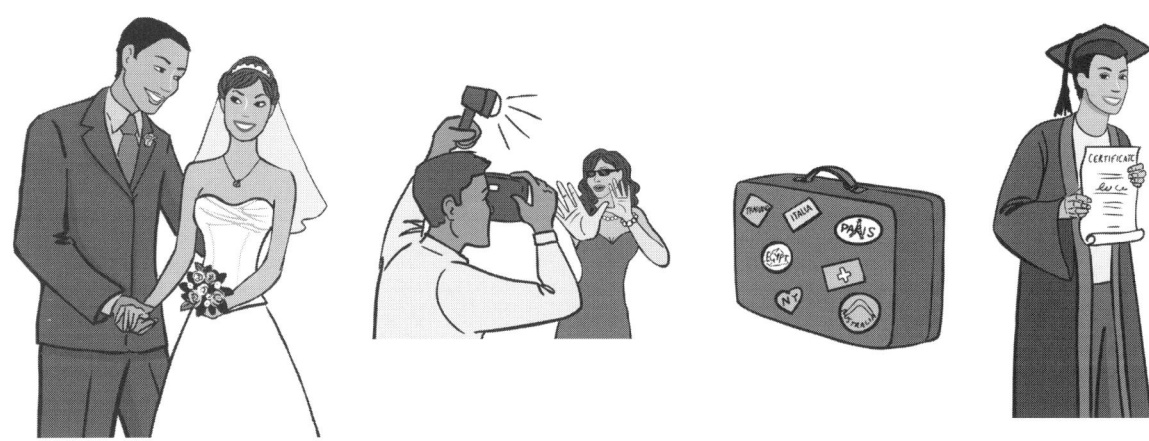

2 Now tell your partner your predictions and answer his/her questions. Listen to your partner's predictions about your future and ask questions to find out extra information.

A: I think you will probably be rich and famous.

B: Will I be a film star?

Student B

1 Look at the pictures and write predictions about your partner's future. Use your imagination!

2 Now tell your partner your predictions and answer his/her questions. Listen to your partner's predictions about your future and ask questions to find out extra information.

B: I think you will probably have a lot of children.

A: Where will I live?

1 Present perfect: questions and short answers

Complete the questions. Use the past participles of the verbs in the box.
Then complete the short answers.

| stop   make   ~~do~~   cut   learn   buy   eat   pass |

1 Has Jill __*done*__ her homework?   No, __*she hasn't*__ .
2 Have your parents _____ a new car?   No, _____ .
3 Have you _____ all the chocolates?   No, _____ .
4 Have you _____ Teresa's birthday cake?   Yes, _____ .
5 Has Tommy _____ his hair?   Yes, _____ .
6 Has it _____ raining?   No, _____ .
7 Has Christine _____ her driving test?   Yes, _____ .
8 Have you _____ all the past participles?   No, _____ .

2 Present perfect: affirmative and negative

Complete the sentences. Use the present perfect affirmative or negative form of the verbs.

1 Sheila __*hasn't gone*__ (not go) to bed. It's only nine o'clock!
2 My physics teacher _____ (write) a book. It's about the stars.
3 You _____ (not turn off) the computer. I'll do it.
4 Dan _____ (read) *Northern Lights* three times. It's his favourite book.
5 We _____ (make) some cakes. Would you like one?
6 You _____ (not eat) all your vegetables. Don't you like them?
7 Dominic _____ (not do) the shopping. He says he'll do it tomorrow.
8 I _____ (bring) you a present. I hope you like it.

3 Present perfect: questions

Write the questions. Use the present perfect.

1 Julian / tidy / his bedroom?
   Has Julian tidied his bedroom?
2 Annie and Ian / change / their phone number?
   _____
3 your sister / find / her rucksack?
   _____

4 you and Lillian / meet / my cousin?
   _____
5 it / stop raining?
   _____
6 you / hear / the new Eminem album?
   _____
7 Jack / buy / a PlayStation?
   _____
8 Ellie / invite / Tania to the barbecue?
   _____

4 Present perfect or past simple?

Complete the sentences. Use the present perfect or past simple form of the verbs.

1 The Pollards don't live here now. They __*have moved*__ (move) to Manchester.
2 _____ (you/see) that new sports programme on TV last night?
3 We _____ (go) to Spain after Christmas.
4 Oh no! I think I _____ (lose) my keys!
5 Jenny's really hungry. She _____ (not/eat) today.
6 Terry's in the garden. I _____ (see) him five minutes ago.
7 You won't believe this – Anna and George _____ (get) married!
8 _____ (you/finish) that book?

Student A

1 Take it in turns to ask and answer questions.

Here is a list of things that Kerry needs to do. Ask your partner if she has done them and put a tick or a cross by each:

A: Has Kerry done the washing up?

B: No, she hasn't.

Kerry's list of things to do:

- do the washing up
- buy some bread
- clean the floor
- do the shopping
- make the coffee

2 This is Christine's bedroom. Listen to your partner's questions about Christine and answer them.

B: Has Christine made the bed?

A: No, she hasn't.

Student B

1 Take it in turns to ask and answer questions.

This is Kerry's kitchen. Listen to your partner's questions about Kerry and answer them.

A: Has Kerry done the washing up?

B: No, she hasn't.

2 Here is a list of things that Christine needs to do. Ask your partner if she has done them and put a tick or a cross by each.

B: Has Christine made the bed?

A: No, she hasn't.

Christine's list of things to do:

- make the bed
- buy Dad's birthday present
- clean the windows
- tidy my room
- do my homework

1 Present perfect + *ever, never* and *just*

Put the words in the right order and make sentences.

1 food / Sally / ever / has / Indian / tried?

   Has Sally ever tried Indian food?

2 the / Holland / World / never / has / won / Cup

   ....

3 Barry / seen / a / has / snake / just !

   ....

4 done / what / Tom / just / has ?

   ....

5 abroad / never / grandfather / been / has / my

   ....

6 a / you / famous / ever / met / person / have ?

   ....

7 China/ been / never / have / I / to

   ....

8 spoken / just / to / have / I / Steve

   ....

2 Present perfect + *for* and *since*

Complete the sentences with *for* or *since*.

1 Felix has lived in Edinburgh ___*since*___ 1998.

2 Mrs Harris has been a teacher .... 12 years.

3 I've known you .... I was four.

4 We've had a DVD player .... February.

5 Pablo hasn't been to the cinema .... ages.

6 This shirt isn't very old. I've only had it .... three weeks.

7 They've had the euro in lots of countries .... 2002.

8 We've been here .... 40 minutes.

3 Time expressions with *for* and *since*

Complete the second sentence so it means the same as the first one. Use *for* and *since*.

1 Dave bought his digital camera on Saturday. It's now Wednesday.

   Dave *has had his digital camera for* five days. (have)

2 Jack's mum and dad got married in 1991.

   Jack's mum and dad ....

   .... 1991. (be married)

3 I met you in 1998. It's now 2005.

   I .... seven years. (know)

4 U2 are my favourite band. I liked them when I first heard them in 1998.

   I .... 1998. (like)

5 Kevin went to live in Birmingham when he was four. He lives there now.

   Kevin .... he was four. (live)

6 My sister is a nurse. She started working ten months ago.

   My sister .... ten months. (be)

4 Present perfect: *How long . . . ?*

Make questions for the sentences in Exercise 3.

1 *How long has Dave had his digital camera?*

2 ....

3 ....

4 ....

5 ....

6 ....

Student A

1 Take it in turns to ask and answer questions.

Read the information about Emma and then answer your partner's questions about her.

B: Has Emma been to university?   A: No, she hasn't.

> Emma left school when she was 18. She decided not to go to university because she wanted to travel. She went to lots of interesting countries like India, Sri Lanka and Thailand, but her favourite place was Latin America. She worked as a waitress in Argentina for six months and met a lot of interesting people. She then decided to work in Spain. She moved there four years ago and she loves it! Two years ago she got a job in a shop in Barcelona. Three months ago, she bought a flat in Sitges, a small town near Barcelona, and she drives to work every day. She lives there with her friend, Maria. Emma would like to go to Egypt for her next holiday because everyone tells her it's very beautiful. Then she hopes to go to university!

2 Your partner has got some information about Joanne. Ask your partner questions to find out if the following sentences are **true** or **false**:

A: Has Joanne travelled a lot?   B: Yes, she has.

1 Joanne has travelled a lot.
2 She's worked on *Belle* magazine for three months.
3 She's never been skiing.
4 She's stayed at a 5 star hotel.
5 She's been to university.

6 She's worked on a national newspaper.
7 She's been married for a year and a half.
8 She's never won a prize.
9 She's finished her article on Prague.
10 She's written about American cities.

Student B

1 Take it in turns to ask and answer questions.

Your partner has got some information about Emma. Ask your partner questions to find out if the following sentences are **true** or **false**.

B: Has Emma been to university?   A: No, she hasn't.

1 Emma's been to university.
2 She hasn't travelled a lot.
3 She's been a waitress for two years.
4 She's lived in Spain for four years.
5 She hasn't passed her driving test.

6 She's eaten Indian food.
7 She's been a teacher.
8 She's been to Egypt.
9 She's lived in her flat for three years.
10 She's met a lot of interesting people.

2 Read the information about Joanne and then answer your partner's questions about her.

A: Has Joanne travelled a lot?   B: Yes, she has.

> After university, Joanne worked for a few local newspapers, then three years ago she got a job on Belle magazine. She writes articles about European cities. In fact, her article about Paris won an important prize! She loves her job because she travels a lot. She usually goes to a European country once a month and she always stays at 5 star hotels. She lives in London with her husband, who also works on the magazine. They got married 18 months ago and they're very happy. They're both very active and they usually go skiing at Christmas. This year they're not going because Joanne's very busy. At the moment, she's working hard because she wants to finish the article she's writing about Prague.

1 *have to* and *don't have to*

Complete the sentences with *have to* / *has to* or *don't* / *doesn't have to*.

1 My sister _doesn't have to_ wear a school uniform. She usually wears jeans.

2 Barbara can't come out tonight. She _____ stay at home with her sister.

3 You _____ go if you don't want to.

4 Paul and Jamie _____ get up early. Their school is quite far from their home.

5 Tomorrow's Saturday – we _____ go to school!

6 A taxi driver _____ know where places are in the city.

7 The doctor says you _____ take the medicine three times a day, before meals.

8 Maria _____ do the washing up. Peter's done it.

2 *don't have to* and *mustn't*

Complete the sentences with *don't* / *doesn't have to* or *mustn't*.

1 You _mustn't_ talk in an exam.

2 You _____ be a great athlete if you want to play table tennis.

3 Catherine _____ take an umbrella because it isn't going to rain.

4 You _____ make lots of noise in the library. People are trying to study.

5 Jim says we _____ use his books if we don't ask him first.

6 You _____ spend lots of money if you want to have a good time.

7 The teacher told Stephanie that she _____ be late again or he'll contact her parents.

8 We _____ go out. We can stay in and watch TV if you like.

3 *should* and *shouldn't*

Here are some problems. Complete the advice with *should* or *shouldn't* and one of the verbs in the box.

> take ~~buy~~ spend go look for
> go out with

1 I'm having problems with my English. You _should buy_ should buy a good grammar book.

2 Tracey's boyfriend is really selfish. She _____ him.

3 Kate's dad works in an office, but he's fed up with his job. He _____ another job.

4 The weather's too cold in England, and it always rains. Yes, we _____ and live in the south of Spain!

5 I hate the food at school. You _____ a packed lunch.

6 Carl can't go bowling with us. He hasn't got enough money. He _____ all his money on clothes.

4 Rules, obligations and advice

Choose the right words.

1 You _____ go to Britain if you want to practise your English.
  a have to b should c mustn't

2 You _____ be 18 if you want to vote in Britain.
  a mustn't b should c have to

3 You _____ be English to speak good English.
  a mustn't b shouldn't c don't have to

4 You _____ tell anyone. It's a secret.
  a mustn't b don't have to c have to

5 Brian _____ get up early tomorrow because it's Sunday.
  a shouldn't b mustn't c doesn't have to

6 You _____ eat too much fast food because it's not good for you.
  a don't have to b shouldn't c must

Student A

Take it in turns to ask your partner about the missing words in your puzzle and to describe the words in your puzzle for your partner.

A: What's 4 across?   B: It's a person who looks after your teeth.

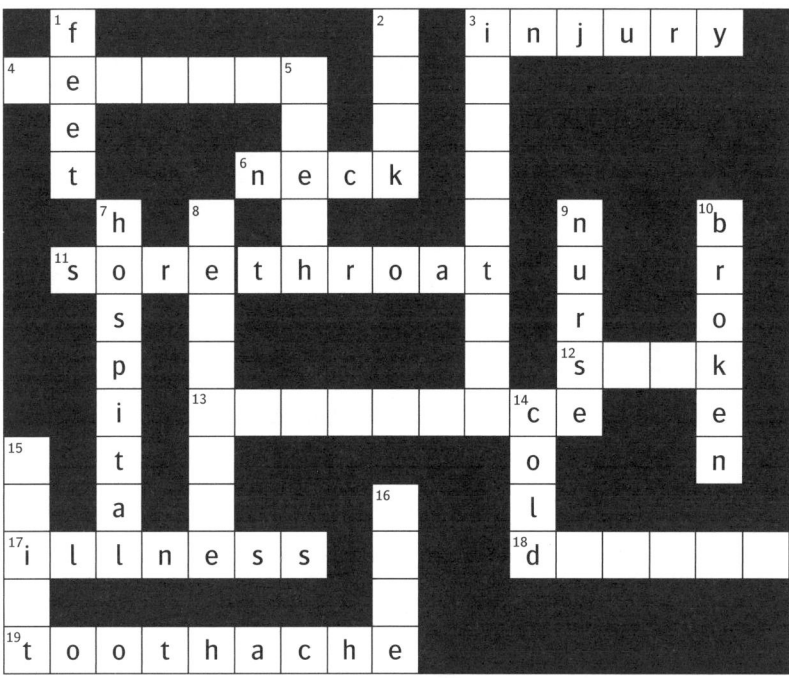

Student B

Take it in turns to ask your partner about the missing words in your puzzle and to describe the words in your puzzle for your partner.

B: What's 1 down?   A: They're the things at the end of your legs.

1 Expressing a reaction

Match the sentences with the reactions (a–h).

1 I finished the exam in 15 minutes!

2 Roy found £50 in the library and he gave it to the librarian.

3 I paid £7.25 for a cup of coffee and a sandwich on the train!

4 My sister has found a job at last!

5 Nick was in a car accident! He's been in hospital for a week.

6 Luke gave me a lot of his old video games last week.

a That's great!

b That's expensive!

c ~~That's fast!~~

d That's terrible!

e That's honest!

f That's generous!

1 _c_   2 _____   3 _____   4 _____   5 _____   6 _____   7 _____   8 _____

2 Present simple passive

Complete the second sentence so that it means the same as the first one. Use the verbs in the passive.

1 They make Volkswagen cars in Germany.

   Volkswagen cars __are made__ in Germany.

2 They speak Spanish in Argentina and Mexico.

   Spanish _____ in Argentina and Mexico.

3 People buy millions of cars every year.

   Millions of cars _____ every year.

4 They serve lunch on the plane.

   Lunch _____ on the plane.

5 They produce champagne in France.

   Champagne _____ in France.

6 His company pays him at the end of every month.

   He _____ at the end of every month.

3 Past simple passive

Complete the sentences. Use the verbs in the past passive.

1 The Mona Lisa __was painted__ (paint) by Leonardo Da Vinci.

2 Those shoes _____ (make) in China.

3 The pyramids _____ (build) in Egypt.

4 In 2000, the Olympics _____ (hold) in Sydney.

5 Television _____ (invent) in 1926.

4 Passive questions

Write the questions, then complete the answers. Use the present simple passive or past simple passive form of the verbs.

1 When / Guernica / paint?

   When was Guernica painted?

   It __was painted__ in 1937.

2 When / these houses / build?

   _____ ?

   They _____ in the 1960s.

3 Which languages / teach / at this school?

   _____ ?

   French and Spanish _____ here.

4 Who / Hamlet / write by?

   _____ ?

   It _____ by Shakespeare.

5 Where / John Lennon / kill?

   _____ ?

   He _____ in New York.

6 Where / bananas / grow?

   _____ ?

   They _____ in Dominica.

		16	17	
Go back to the start.	When / *Toy Story* / release?	Where / the Statue of Liberty / make?	FINISH	

15	14	13	
When / the first computer game / create?	Who / *Sunflowers* / paint by?	Where / the first lift / use?	Miss a turn.

	10	11	12
Throw the dice again.	Who / *Somewhere over the rainbow* / sing by?	When / *Snow White and the Seven Dwarfs* / make?	Where / the first Olympic Games / hold?

9	8	7	
Which US president / assassinate in 1963?	When / the Eiffel Tower / build?	Who / *Guernica* / paint by?	Go back 2 squares.

	4	5	6
Go forward 2 squares.	Where / the first skyscraper / build?	When / the first lift / use?	Which Disney cartoon character / create in 1928?

3	2	1	
Who / the *Star Wars* films / direct by?	What / the first computer game / call?	When / *The Wizard of Oz* / make?	START

1 *say* or *tell*?

Complete the sentences. Use the right form of *say* or *tell*.

1 Lynne ___told___ me your sister was better now. That's great news!

2 Did Paul _____ he was going cycling on Sunday?

3 Karen always _____ her parents about her problems.

4 Andy and Jack _____ they didn't want to eat pasta.

5 No, I _____ I couldn't go.

6 Lee _____ Tony that he went to the gym every day. That's not true!

7 Why did Michael _____ you he was at the cinema?

8 Julie _____ she wasn't worried about the exam.

2 Reported speech

Look for a mistake in each sentence. Underline the mistake and correct it.

1 'I meet my little brother after school every day.'
Kenny said he met <u>my</u> little brother after school every day.
___*his*___

2 'I don't like your new dress.'
Elaine said Sarah that she didn't like her new dress.
_____

3 'Helen is my closest friend.'
Kelly told that Helen was her closest friend.
_____

4 'You're really clever!'
Mr Graves told me that I were really clever.
_____

5 'My brother has got a headache.'
Annie said her brother got a headache.
_____

6 'We go skiing every weekend in the winter.'
Don and Zak said we went skiing every weekend in the winter.
_____

3 Reported speech

Complete the sentences. Use reported speech.

1 'I'm really tired!'
Sonia said ___she was really tired___ .

2 'I've got a lot of homework.'
Benny said _____
_____ .

3 'I can't find my keys.'
John told Maria _____
_____ .

4 'I'm not the tallest person in my class.'
Tina said _____
_____ .

5 'We leave home at 7.30 every morning.'
Jim and Dawn said _____
_____ .

6 'I don't argue with my sister.'
Fiona said _____
_____ .

7 'My mum and dad are at the supermarket.'
Patrick said _____
_____ .

8 'I love you.'
Karen told me _____
_____ .

4 Question tags

Complete the question tags.

1 Your brother lives in Italy, ___*doesn't*___ he?

2 That new girl isn't very friendly, _____ she?

3 Paul can swim, _____ he?

4 You go to my school, _____ you?

5 Your friends weren't very pleased, _____ they?

6 Your dad is a mechanic, _____ he?

7 Sally didn't drink all the milk, _____ she?

8 I'll see you tomorrow, _____ I?

9 You aren't coming, _____ you?

10 It wasn't very interesting, _____ it?

Student A

1 Here is a picture of some people at a party. Ask your partner what the people said and fill in the empty speech bubbles with direct speech.

A: What did Helen say?

2 Now answer your partner's questions using reported speech.

B: What did Pete say?   A: He said he didn't like tomatoes.

Student B

1 Here is a picture of some people at a party. Answer your partner's questions using reported speech.

A: What did Helen say?   B: She said she could speak Japanese.

2 Now ask your partner what the other people said and fill in the empty speech bubbles with direct speech.

B: What did Pete say?

1 used to

Rewrite the sentences with *used to* or *didn't use to*.

1 I thought basketball was boring until I went to a match. Now I really like it.

   I _didn't use to like_ basketball.

2 I lived in New York before I came to live here.

   I _____ in New York.

3 My mum stopped smoking two years ago.

   My mum _____ .

4 What's the matter with Keith? Why is he so moody?

   Keith _____ so moody.

5 I didn't like English until I went to Britain. Now I'm really interested in it!

   I _____ interested in English.

6 Lucy had to start wearing a uniform when she started her new school.

   Lucy _____ a uniform to school.

2 Second conditional: questions and short answers

Complete the questions with the correct form of the verbs in the box. Then complete the answers.

live	~~win~~	give	catch	go	play	use	be

1 A: Would you give all your money to charity if you _won_ the lottery?

   B: No, _I wouldn't_ .

2 A: Would it be OK if I _____ to the cinema with Traccy tonight?

   B: Yes, _____ .

3 A: Would Alison mind if I _____ her bike?

   B: No, _____ .

4 A: Would I speak American English if I _____ in America?

   B: Yes, _____ .

5 A: Would Dad be annoyed if I _____ my saxophone?

   B: Yes, _____ .

6 A: Would it be quicker if we _____ the train?

   B: No, _____ .

7 A: Would you be happy if you _____ rich?

   B: Yes, _____ .

8 A: Would you call me if I _____ you my phone number?

   B: Yes, _____ .

3 Second conditional

Complete the sentences, using the second conditional.

1 If I _was_ (be) the president, the world _would be_ (be) a better place.

2 If I _____ (meet) David Beckham, I _____ (be) very nervous.

3 If you _____ (study) more, you _____ (not need) to repeat your exams.

4 If Carol _____ (not be) so rude, more people _____ (like) her.

5 If Ian _____ (not cut) his hair so short, he _____ (be) more good-looking.

6 If Janine _____ (help) me, we _____ (finish) more quickly.

4 Second conditional

Rewrite these sentences using the second conditional.

1 Johnny won't buy a new computer because he hasn't got enough money.

   If Johnny _had enough money,_ _he'd buy_ a new computer.

2 I don't live in the USA so I don't play baseball.

   If I _____ baseball.

3 This tea is very hot. I'll drink it later.

   If the tea _____ _____ it now.

4 You don't do any exercise. That's why you're always tired.

   If you _____ so tired all the time.

5 I won't go to Brazil in the summer because I can't speak Portuguese.

   If I _____ to Brazil in the summer.

What would *you* do?

Make sentences to describe each picture. Then ask and answer questions about you.

A: What would you do if you were invisible?

B: I would ...

1   if Paul / be invisible / not pay to go to the cinema

2   if Mary / win the lottery / buy a new car

3   if Sally / not have to go to school / watch TV all day

4   if Dave / can travel in time / travel to the 1960s

5   if Kerry / be head teacher at her school / the teachers / have to wear uniforms

1 Grammar

a Complete the sentences. Circle the right answer: a, b or c.

0 A: Do you know my sister?

   B: ....

   a Yes, she does.   b Yes, I know.   ⓒ Yes, I do.

1 A: .... are you from?

   B: I'm from New York.

   a Where   b What   c Who

2 A: Were Amy and Megan at school yesterday?

   B: ....

   a No, they weren't.   b No, they aren't.

   c No, they didn't.

3 A: .... John angry?

   B: Yes, he is.

   a Are   b Is   c Am

4 A: .... did you buy?

   B: Some jeans.

   a What   b When   c How

5 A: Do you feel homesick?

   B: ....

   a Yes, she does.   b Yes, I do.   c No, they don't.

6 A: .... she come from Paris?

   B: Yes, she does.

   a Do   b Is   c Does

7 A: Did your brother enjoy the party?

   B: ....

   a Yes, she did.   b Yes, he was.   c Yes, he did.

8 A: .... they got any friends in London?

   B: Yes, they've got a lot.

   a Have   b Do   c Does

9 A: Was it raining when you came home?

   B: ....

   a Yes, it was.   b Yes, he was.   c Yes, I was.

10 A: ....'s that boy over there?

   B: He's my brother.

   a Where   b Who   c When

   [10]

b Complete the sentences with the right form of the verbs in the box. Choose between the present continuous or the present simple.

| have study play stay speak |
| not understand |

0 We always _have_ a really good time at Luke's house.

1 A: Where's Lucy?

   B: She .... for her French test upstairs.

2 Listen! Lee .... his guitar. He's really good!

3 Can you say that again? I ....

4 In Canada a lot of people .... French.

5 I .... with a family in Chester at the moment.

Now choose between the past continuous and the past simple.

| not meet   sink   wait   go   play |

6 Ben .... football with his friends when it started to rain.

7 The boat hit a large rock and .... really quickly.

8 Katie .... Dan yesterday – she was ill.

9 Tom and Josh .... outside the cinema when Tom's mobile phone rang.

10 Ana and Jay .... into the shop and bought a book.

   [10]

   Grammar [20]

MODULE 1 TEST   UNITS 1–2

2 Vocabulary

Name

Class   Date

a Read the sentences. Circle the right answer: a, b or c.

0 It was the 6th of December ...... Alex was staying with some friends in the Lake District.

   a after   (b) and   c before

1 They were going upstairs to bed ...... they heard a loud noise.

   a suddenly   b when   c before

2 They were scared ...... they decided to go downstairs and check the rooms.

   a then   b after   c but

3 ...... they opened the kitchen door, they couldn't see anything.

   a When   b But   c Suddenly

4 ...... something small and black appeared and ran into the living room! It was the family cat.

   a And   b Suddenly   c After

5 ...... they realised this, they all started laughing.

   a When   b But   c And

5

b Write the countries and nationalities.

0 Japan   *Japanese*

1 Mexico   ....

2 .... Australian

3 Greece   ....

4 .... Polish

5 The USA   ....

5

c Write the numbers in words.

0 36,000,000   *thirty-six million*

1 4½   ....

2 3.25   ....

3 76%   ....

4 ¾   ....

5 596   ....

6 8¼   ....

7 200,000,000   ....

8 12½   ....

9 6,385   ....

10 7.63   ....

10

Vocabulary   20

Messages 3 PHOTOCOPIABLE © Cambridge University Press 2006   Module 1 test

3 Reading

The people below are planning their holidays.
Choose the country that is the best for each of them.

①

Jamie likes visiting museums when he's on holiday. His favourite subjects at school are art and history and he loves looking at paintings.

②

Hannah loves activity holidays and wants to go to the mountains with a group of friends. She only speaks English and wants to go to an English-speaking country.

③

William's idea of a good holiday is sun, sea and sand. He's happy to spend all day on the beach with a good book. In the evening he likes dancing and talking to the local people.

④

Matt doesn't live by the sea, but he recently started surfing. He loves it and wants to go a place where the surfing is good.

⑤

Michaela is learning English and she wants to go to a country where she can practise it. She's studying Shakespeare at school and is very interested in his life.

e

Enjoy a holiday in Australia!
Spend your days on Bondi Beach riding the waves, and your evenings in downtown Sydney trying our amazing food!

f

Canada is a land of mountains, lakes and forests.

It's the perfect holiday destination for people who love walking. Autumn is the best time to visit: cool temperatures, great views, clean air.

A true paradise on Earth!

a

Argentina, between the Andes to the west and the Atlantic Ocean to the east, is full of surprises. You can dance the tango in Buenos Aires or climb Mount Aconcagua, the highest mountain in the Americas. You will want to come back again and again.

c

Leonardo da Vinci, Michelangelo and Raphael: Italy is the home of Renaissance art. We know you will have a fantastic holiday here.

g

Come to the Newton Language School and you'll see that the people and the weather in England aren't always cold!

Improve your English and learn about British culture. We offer classes and cultural trips for teenagers and adults.

b

THERE'S SOMETHING FOR EVERYONE IN AMERICA.

Meet your favourite Disney characters, see a musical on Broadway, visit a Hollywood film set or enjoy the wonderful national parks. And don't forget the fantastic shopping centres!

d

THE PERFECT PLACE
...for a relaxing beach holiday is Greece. The sea is warm, the sand is golden, the sky is blue and the sun always shines! After a day on the beach, you can meet new people in a *taverna* and then dance all night under the stars.

1 _____ 2 _____

3 _____ 4 _____ 5 _____

Reading | 10

MODULE 1 TEST   UNITS 1–2

4 Writing

Read this email from Jack.

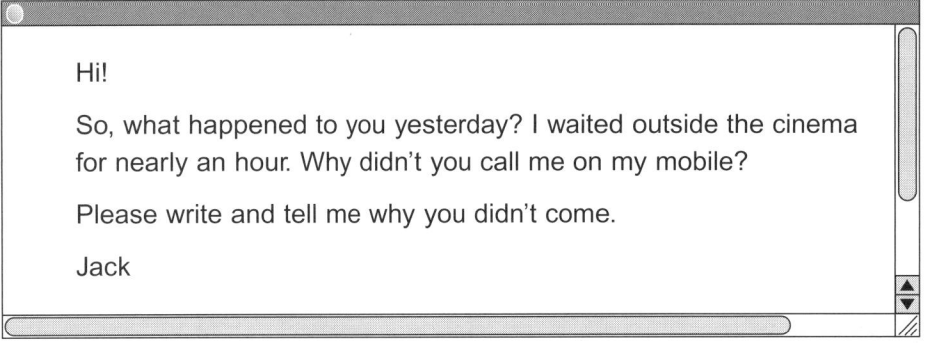

Hi!

So, what happened to you yesterday? I waited outside the cinema for nearly an hour. Why didn't you call me on my mobile?

Please write and tell me why you didn't come.

Jack

Answer Jack's email. Apologise and explain why you didn't meet him. Write 25–35 words.

| Writing | 10 |

5 Listening 🔊 Class CD 1 Track 21

a 📻 You will hear someone talking about the famous ship the *Titanic*.
For each question fill in the missing information.

1 The *Titanic* left Southampton on 10th April _____ .

2 There were _____ passengers.

3 The ship hit an iceberg on Sunday, _____ .

4 It sank at _____ a.m.

5 _____ people died.

b 📻 You will hear a conversation between Harry and Emma.
Are sentences 1–5 true (T) or false (F)?
Tick (✓) the right answer.

1 It's eight o'clock.   T _____ F _____
2 Emma is happy to see Harry.   T _____ F _____
3 Harry missed his bus.   T _____ F _____
4 Harry forgot his phone.   T _____ F _____
5 Emma wants to go for a pizza. T _____ F _____

Listening	10
Speaking	10
Test total	80

Please note that the audio material for the Listening test is on the Class Cassettes/CDs.

6 Speaking

a Two students answer your questions.

- Greet Students A and B and ask them how they are.

- Ask each student questions connected with the past. For example: *What did you do at the weekend? Where did you go for your last summer holiday?* (This is to practise the past simple.)

b Two students talk to each other.

- Explain that the students are going to ask each other questions about their primary school, using the prompts on the cards. Give Student A the prompt card A and give Student B the prompt card B. They should take it in turns to ask each other their questions.

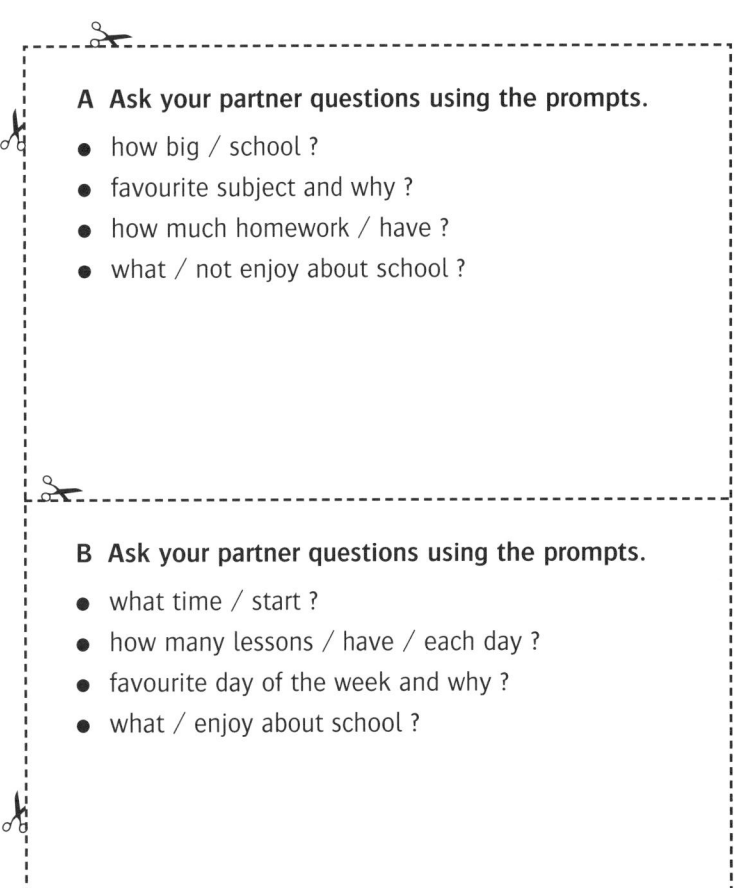

A Ask your partner questions using the prompts.

- how big / school ?
- favourite subject and why ?
- how much homework / have ?
- what / not enjoy about school ?

B Ask your partner questions using the prompts.

- what time / start ?
- how many lessons / have / each day ?
- favourite day of the week and why ?
- what / enjoy about school ?

1 Grammar

a 1 a 2 a 3 b 4 a 5 b 6 c 7 c 8 a
9 a 10 b

b 1 's/is studying 2 's/is playing
3 don't understand 4 speak 5 'm/am staying
6 was playing 7 sank 8 didn't meet
9 were waiting 10 went

2 Vocabulary

a 1 b 2 c 3 a 4 b 5 a

b 1 Mexican 2 Australia 3 Greek
4 Poland 5 American

c 1 four and a half
2 three point two five
3 seventy-six percent
4 three quarters
5 five hundred and ninety-six
6 eight and a quarter
7 two hundred million
8 twelve and half
9 six thousand three hundred and eighty-five
10 seven point six three

3 Reading

1 c 2 f 3 d 4 e 5 g

4 Writing

Check individual answers.

5 Listening

a

Tapescript

The story of the ship the *Titanic* is famous, and the film of what happened was a big success. The *Titanic* left Southampton, England on 10th April, 1912. It was sailing to New York with 2,208 passengers. It was the *Titanic*'s first journey and there were many rich and famous people on the ship. On the night of Sunday, 14th April, the ship hit an iceberg and started to sink. At first, no one realised what was happening. The ship finally sank at 2.20 a.m. 1,523 people died on that terrible night.

1 1912 2 2,208 3 14th April
4 2.20 a.m. 5 1,523

b

Tapescript

EMMA: So what happened? Where were you? It's eight o'clock! Why didn't you phone me?

HARRY: I'm sorry. I know I'm late but it wasn't my fault.

EMMA: I don't believe you. This isn't the first time, you know!

HARRY: Honestly, the bus was early – that's why I missed it – and I couldn't find a taxi.

EMMA: OK, but why didn't you phone?

HARRY: I left my phone at home.

EMMA: Great! So why have you got a mobile phone then?

HARRY: Look, I'm here now – so let's go for a pizza.

EMMA: No, I don't want to. I think I'll go home.

HARRY: Come on, Emma! Don't be silly… !

1 T 2 F 3 T 4 T 5 F

6 Speaking

Check individual answers.

1 Grammar

a Complete the sentences. Circle the right answer: a, b or c.

0 There are ...... cars on the roads today.

 a too much   b a lot   ⓒ too many

1 You're very different ...... your sister.

 a from   b by   c of

2 A: What ...... your uncle like?

 B: He's really nice.

 a has   b is   c does

3 Oh no! I haven't got ...... money to buy this CD.

 a enough   b a lot of   c too much

4 Katie is ...... popular girl in our class.

 a more   b most   c the most

5 I don't like geography very much, but my ...... subject is maths!

 a worst   b bad   c worse

6 How about ...... for a pizza this evening?

 a go   b to go   c going

7 This soup is disgusting! You put ...... pepper in it.

 a too many   b too much   c enough

8 I'm sorry I can't come out later – I've got ...... homework.

 a a lot of   b enough   c too many

9 Do you think Brad Pitt is as good-looking ...... Leonardo di Caprio?

 a than   b to   c as

10 ...... your brother really look like Tom Cruise?

 a Has   b Does   c Is

[10]

b Complete the second sentence so that it means the same as the first. Use no more than three words.

0 English is easier than German.

 German isn't _as easy as_ English.

1 David isn't as confident as Max.

 Max is .... David.

2 Josh is better at maths than Nick.

 Nick isn't .... at maths .... Josh.

3 Everything on the menu is cheaper than the steak.

 The steak is .... thing on the menu.

4 Rebecca is 1.68 m and Sophie is 1.69 m.

 Sophie is .... Rebecca.

5 I don't know anyone who is lazier than you!

 You are .... person I know!

[10]

| Grammar | 20 |

2 Vocabulary

a Complete the sentences using the words in the box.

| adventurous shy ~~clever~~ unhealthy easy-going |
| generous unpopular unkind lazy moody unhappy |

0 Alex is very __*clever*__ . He always knows all the answers.

1 The prime minister is very _____ at the moment. No one seems to like him.

2 Lucy is very _____ . She never tidies her room or helps at home.

3 Megan went hiking in the Himalayas last year. She's very _____ . She often goes to new places.

4 What's the matter with Josh? He's so _____ . One day he's happy and the next day he's sad.

5 Max is very _____ sometimes. He says some very cruel things.

6 Libby is very _____ . She never speaks to people she doesn't know.

7 Peter eats too much fast food. I'm not surprised that he's _____ .

8 My grandparents are very _____ . They bought me a fantastic computer for my birthday.

9 Our history teacher is _____ . She never gets angry with us!

10 Why are you crying? Don't be _____ . Everything will be fine.

| 10 |

b What are these places? Put the letters in the right order and make words.

0 estalc __*castle*__

1 clapea _____

2 meeth karp _____

3 mudtasi _____

4 talrached _____

5 quomse _____

6 tar lagreyl _____

7 plemet _____

8 maruquai _____

9 retathe _____

10 trapemtend retos _____

| 10 |

| Vocabulary | 20 |

Read the text.

Name ....

Class .... Date ....

MOSCOW

Moscow is the capital of Russia and is on the river Moskva. It is a huge city with a population of 11.2 million. It is, perhaps surprisingly, the most expensive city in Europe and the second most expensive city in the world after Tokyo. It is also the city with the most billionaires in the world; in 2004 it had 33, two more than New York City.

Things to see

There is something for everyone; famous places include the Kremlin, Red Square with the onion domes of St Basil's Cathedral, the Zoo, the Bolshoi Theatre with its world-famous ballet company and the Ostankino Tower (a television and radio tower) – Moscow's tallest building at 577 metres. Winter, when the streets are under snow, is definitely the best time to visit this beautiful city. It can be extremely cold, with temperatures as low as –25 degrees Celsius, but it is very romantic.

Transport

There are four airports. Moscow also has the world's busiest metro system. It began in 1935 and now has 11 lines with more than 150 stations. Many of them have art and mosaics and look like museums. Nine million passengers use the metro every day and there are trains every 50 seconds during the busiest times. There are two international airports.

Moscow is an exciting, lively city with so much to offer. Come and see for yourself. You'll love it!

Are these sentences true (T) or false (F)? Tick (✓) the right answer.

1 There isn't a river in Moscow.   T .... F ....
2 Tokyo is the most expensive city in the world.   T .... F ....
3 New York has 35 billionaires.   T .... F ....
4 You can go to a ballet at the Bolshoi Theatre.   T .... F ....
5 Moscow is very romantic in winter.   T .... F ....
6 The Ostankino Tower is very high.   T .... F ....
7 The metro isn't very popular.   T .... F ....
8 There is one train every minute, even during the night.   T .... F ....
9 You can fly to Moscow.   T .... F ....
10 Moscow is a great city to visit.   T .... F ....

| Reading | 10 |

4 Writing

Write an email to your pen friend, Maria, and tell her about your favourite place.
In your email, you should say

● where your favourite place is

● why you like it

● how often you go there.

Write 35–45 words.

| Writing | 10 |

MODULE 2 TEST   UNITS 3–4

5 Listening 🔊 Class CD 1 Track 40

Name
Class _____ Date _____

a 📻 For each question there are three pictures. Listen and then choose the correct picture and put a tick (✓) in the box below it.

1 Which boy is Ben?

a  **b**  **c**

2 Which girl is Sarah?

a  **b**  **c**

3 Which is the most expensive place to visit?

a  **b**  **c**

4 Which country has the largest number of people?

a 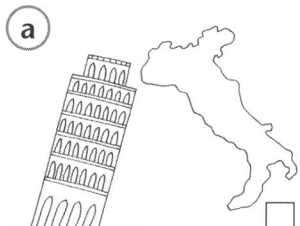 **b**  **c**

5 Which dog is Max's?

a  **b**  **c**

b 📻 Listen to Abby and Tom's telephone conversation. Are sentences 1–5 true (T) or false (F)? Tick (✓) the right answer.

1 Abby thinks Tom is good at exams. T _____ F _____
2 Abby has got some tickets for a concert on Sunday. T _____ F _____
3 Tom would like to go for a coffee before the concert. T _____ F _____
4 Tom and Abby are going to meet at 5 o'clock. T _____ F _____
5 Abby says that Tom is normally late. T _____ F _____

Listening	10
Speaking	10
Test total	80

Please note that the audio material for the Listening test is on the Class Cassettes/CDs.

6 Speaking

a Two students answer your questions.

- Greet Students A and B and ask them how they are.

- Ask each student about their city/town. For example: *Which part of town do you live in? Which is your favourite place in town? Where do you usually go at the weekends?*

b Two students talk to each other.

- Explain that some friends are coming to stay for a few days and they have never visited the students' capital city before. Students A and B should talk together and decide which three places shown in the pictures they would most like to take their friends to. They should take it in turns to make suggestions. When Student A makes a suggestion, Student B should agree or disagree, giving reasons. Encourage the students to make full use of the language of suggestion. For example: *Shall we … ? Let's … . How about … ? Why don't we … ?*, etc.

1 Grammar

a 1 a 2 b 3 a 4 c 5 a 6 c 7 b 8 a
     9 c 10 b

b 1 more confident than 2 as good ... as
     3 the most expensive 4 taller than
     5 the laziest

2 Vocabulary

a 1 unpopular 2 lazy 3 adventurous 4 moody
     5 unkind 6 shy 7 unhealthy 8 generous
     9 easy-going 10 unhappy

b 1 palace 2 theme park 3 stadium
     4 cathedral 5 mosque 6 art gallery 7 temple
     8 aquarium 9 theatre 10 department store

3 Reading

1 F 2 T 3 F 4 T 5 T 6 T 7 F 8 F 9 T
10 T

4 Writing

Check individual answers.

5 Listening

a

Tapescript

1 Ben really looks like his dad now. He's got the same
   hair and the same smile. He isn't as tall but I'm sure
   he soon will be. I think they look like brothers!

2 Look at these old photographs of my cousins. Emily
   had long hair, longer than Sally's, but Sarah had the
   longest hair in the family. She was very pretty when
   she was young.

3 It costs £8 to go to the castle, £4 to go to the museum
   and £20 to go to the theme park. Why don't we go to
   the castle – it isn't as expensive as the theme park and
   I'm sure it'll be very interesting.

4 Did you know that the population of the United
   Kingdom is 59,512,000? The population of Italy and
   France is nearly as big. There are 57,840,000 people in
   Italy and 59,330,000 people in France. Where do they
   all live?

5 I'm quite scared of Max's dog. It's big and black and
   it's got very big teeth. It looks much more dangerous
   than my dog – mine is small and white and really
   friendly.

1 c 2 a 3 a 4 b 5 b

b

Tapescript

ABBY: Hi Tom, it's Abby. How are you?

TOM: Hi Abby. I'm fine now because I finished all
     my exams last week.

ABBY: I'm sure you did really well. Listen, I'm
     calling because I've got two tickets for a
     Coldplay concert next Saturday. I know they're
     your favourite band so how about coming
     with me?

TOM: Wow! That's fantastic. I'd love to. Why don't
     we meet in the afternoon and we'll go for a
     coffee or something?

ABBY: That sounds great. Let's meet at 4 o'clock
     outside the station and then we can find a café
     somewhere.

TOM: That sounds good to me. Four o'clock then
     and don't be late.

ABBY: You're the one who's usually late.

TOM: Yeah, yeah ... see you on Saturday then.

ABBY: OK. Bye.

1 T 2 F 3 T 4 F 5 T

6 Speaking

Check individual answers.

1 Grammar

a Complete the sentences with the correct form of the verbs in the box
(present continuous, *going to, will/won't*).

| work   go   hear   not do   ~~meet~~   help   not come   not have   buy   look   have |

0 Who _are_ you _meeting_ after school?

1 I _____ really hard next year because
I want to pass all my exams.

2 Rachel _____ to your house if you
don't invite her.

3 Lizzie's looking round the shops. She
_____ a T-shirt for Martin.

4 We _____ swimming on Saturday.
Do you want to come?

5 A: I can't do this. It's too difficult.

B: Don't worry. I _____ you.

6 If you shout, everyone _____ you.

7 Toby _____ a party on Saturday
because it's his birthday.

8 I think I'll have a starter, but I
_____ a dessert.

9 What _____ mobile phones
_____ like in five years?

10 I can see you at the weekend because
I _____ anything.

[ ] 10

b Put the words in the right order and make sentences.

0 to / evening / the / I'll / cinema / this / go / probably

I'll probably go to the cinema this evening _____ .

1 after / you / able / will / school / be / to / me / meet

Will _____ ?

2 university / study / will / Dan / probably / maths / at

Dan _____ .

3 we / won't / if / play / rains / tennis / it

If _____ .

4 will / every / good / Sam / day / running / if / be / trains / he / at

Sam _____ .

5 year / holiday / we / going / this / on / aren't

We _____ .

6 well / able / German / I'll / speak / be / never / to

I'll _____ !

7 move / going / the / bigger / Browns / to / are / a / house / to

The _____ .

8 I'll / bread / if / have / I / get / time / some

If _____ .

9 let's / not / this / I'm / anything / go / doing / out / evening / so

I'm _____ .

10 if / won't / he's / us / busy / help / he

He _____ .

Grammar [ ] 10

Grammar [ ] 20

2 Vocabulary

Name _____

Class _____ Date _____

a Complete the sentences. Circle the right answer: a, b or c.

0 Excuse me, I'd like to try these trousers _____ .

a in (b) on   c out

1 Mark loves _____ but he doesn't often win them.

a competitors   b computer   c competitions

2 My sister's really afraid _____ spiders.

a of   b about   c at

3 I'll just have a main _____ because I'm not very hungry.

a dish   b course   c plate

4 Use your small _____ for the butter.

a spoon   b knife   c fork

5 Where's the _____ room please? I'd like to try this skirt on.

a living   b waiting   c fitting

6 Don't worry _____ your results. I'm sure they'll be really good.

a about   b for   c at

7 Could you _____ me the bread please, Megan?

a eat   b pass   c take

8 She's very _____ . She wants to win an Olympic medal.

a achieved   b ambitious   c success

9 When the team goes to a different town, they usually travel by _____ .

a airport   b fly   c coach

10 I'm sorry I'm late but there was a terrible _____ jam in the town centre. We didn't move for half an hour.

a car   b bus   c traffic

☐ 10

b Sports. Complete the sentences.

0 Andy Roddick is a great _tennis_ player.

1 If you want to go surfing, you'll need a w _ _ _ _ _ _ .

2 In the winter I always train in a t _ _ _ _ _ _ _ _ because it's very cold.

3 Tony wears g _ _ _ _ _ _ when he swims so he can open his eyes under water.

4 You can e _ _ _ _ the competition if you are under eighteen.

5 Can I wear your b _ _ _ _ ? Your feet are the same size as mine.

6 It's important to wear warm s _ _ _ _ when you go walking in winter.

7 She won a m _ _ _ _ in the competition last year.

8 Matt wants to get some new s _ _ _ _ _ _ _ t _ _ _ _ _ before he goes to the beach.

9 Lisa can't go swimming because she hasn't got her s _ _ _ _ _ _ _ with her.

10 I usually wear s _ _ _ _ _ for football practice because I get too hot in a tracksuit.

☐ 10

| Vocabulary | 20 |

3 Reading

Read the article about Ian Thorpe.

IAN 'THORPEDO' THORPE
– Australian swimming superstar.

Ian James Thorpe was born on 13 October 1982 in Sydney, Australia. His father, Ken, was a successful cricket player but Ian wasn't very good at it. Like his sister, Christina, Ian preferred swimming.

In 1997, at the age of 14, he was the youngest swimmer in the Australian team. He won a silver medal in the Pan Pacific Games in Japan. In 1999 he was the Australian Swimmer of the Year. He won five medals at the 2000 Olympics in Sydney and four medals at the 2004 Olympics in Athens.

He trains for 35 hours every week. He gets up at 4.15 from Monday to Friday and gets to the swimming pool at 5 o'clock. He listens to the radio on his way to the pool and when he swims, he remembers the last song he heard. Sometimes he sings the song in his head all day.

Thorpedo is a very large man! He is 1.95 m tall, weighs 105 kg and wears size 17 shoes! But he's very interested in clothes. He earns millions of pounds a year from companies like *Armani*, *Adidas* and *Omega*.

Many experts say that Ian Thorpe is the greatest swimmer in the world, but he says his ambition is 'to be the best swimmer I can possibly be'.

Are these statements true (T) or false (F)? Tick (✓) the right answer.

1	Ian's father was also a sportsman.	T	F ....
2	His sister, Christina, was a good swimmer.	T	F ....
3	Ian didn't win any competitions in 1999.	T	F ....
4	He gets up at 4.15 seven days a week.	T	F ....
5	He arrives at the pool at 5 o'clock.	T	F ....
6	He listens to music when he swims.	T	F ....
7	Ian Thorpe is very tall.	T	F ....
8	He earns a lot of money from famous companies.	T	F ....
9	A lot of people think he's the greatest swimmer in the world.	T	F ....
10	He wants to be the best swimmer in the world.	T	F ....

Reading	10

MODULE 3 TEST

UNITS 5–6

4 Writing

Your teacher has asked you to write about someone you admire.

You should say

- who this person is and where he/she comes from
- what he/she does
- why you admire him/her

Write 35–45 words.

| Writing | 10 |

5 Listening 🔘 Class CD 1 Track 60

a 📻 Listen to part of a radio programme giving tips on travelling in Africa.

Are sentences 1–5 true (T) or false (F)?
Tick (✓) the right answer.

1	A lot of people go to Africa to see the wild animals.	T	F ....
2	There probably won't be many mosquitoes.	T	F ....
3	A bottle of water is the best thing to drink.	T	F ....
4	You can send emails from all the villages.	T	F ....
5	It is a good idea to learn some local words.	T	F ....

b 📻 **Listen to part of an interview with Bob Bolton, a young professional runner. Answer the questions below.**

1 Which event is Bob going to enter later this year?

....

2 Why is Bob feeling positive?

....

3 What time does Bob wake up every day?

....

4 Who cooks Bob's food?

....

5 What is Bob's ambition?

....

Listening	10
Speaking	10
Test total	80

Please note that the audio material for the Listening test is on the Class Cassettes/CDs.

6 Speaking

a Two students answer your questions.

- Greet Students A and B and ask them how they are.

- Ask each student questions connected with going abroad to study for a term. For example: *Would you like to go to another country to study? What do you think you might miss? What will/might you take with you?*

b Two students talk to each other.

- Explain that a group of students from England is coming to their school on an exchange programme in the summer term. Students A and B should talk together about the things the students might need for their stay and decide which are the most important things to bring with them. The students should use the picture sheet, discuss their ideas with one another and say what they think they will like/not like at their new school. (Encourage them to use *will/won't/probably/might*/first conditional.)

Messages 3   PHOTOCOPIABLE   © Cambridge University Press 2006   Module 3 test

1 Grammar

a 1 'm/am going to work 2 won't come
3 's/is going to buy 4 're/are going
('re going to go) 5 'll/will help 6 'll/will
hear 7 's/is having ('s going to have)
8 won't have 9 will ... look
10 'm/am not doing

b

1 Will you be able to meet me after school?
2 Dan will probably study maths at university.
3 If it rains we won't play tennis.
4 Sam will be good at running if he trains every day.
5 We aren't going on holiday this year.
6 I'll never be able to speak German well!
7 The Browns are going to move to a bigger house.
8 If I have time, I'll get some bread.
9 I'm not doing anything this evening so let's go out.
10 He won't help us if he's busy.

2 Vocabulary

a 1 c 2 a 3 b 4 b 5 c 6 a 7 b 8 b
9 c 10 c

b 1 wetsuit 2 tracksuit 3 goggles 4 enter
5 boots 6 socks 7 medal 8 swimming
trunks 9 swimsuit 10 shorts

3 Reading

1 T 2 T 3 F 4 F 5 T 6 F 7 T 8 T
9 T 10 F

4 Writing

Check individual answers.

5 Listening

a

Tapescript

Africa is a fantastic continent – there are so many places to visit and of course a lot of people go there because they want to see the wild animals. If you're thinking of having a holiday there, then here's some advice. There will probably be a lot of mosquitoes so it's important to take malaria tablets with you. The food will probably be very different so be careful about what you eat. And it's best to drink mineral water if you can. I'm sure you will want to see as much as possible but it's probably better if you don't travel alone. You might feel homesick if you're away for a long time, but, don't worry, you can send emails from the bigger towns. Always tell your family where you're going, then they'll be able to contact you if there's a problem. Try to learn a few words of the local language, for example, 'Hello' in Swahili is 'Jambo!' If you follow this advice, I'm sure you'll have a wonderful time!

1 T 2 F 3 T 4 F 5 T

b

Tapescript

INTERVIEWER: I know you're very busy training, Bob, but can you tell us about your plans for this year?

BOB: Well, as you know, it's the European Championships later this year and I'm going to enter the 400 metres. It'll be my first international event but I'm feeling very positive because I've got a fantastic new trainer.

INTERVIEWER: That's great news. So how do you prepare for these international competitions?

BOB: Well, I train every day of course, in the gym and on the track. I'm bad at getting up early but my trainer always calls me at six o'clock and I'm ready to start training at seven.

INTERVIEWER: How important is food?

BOB: Oh, it's very important. My mum cooks really healthy food and, as you can imagine, I can eat a lot after a day's training!

INTERVIEWER: One last question, Bob. What are your plans after the Championships?

BOB: I hope one day I'll be World Champion. That's what every sports person wants.

INTERVIEWER: Well, good luck and thank you for coming in to talk to us.

1 He's going to enter the 400 metres for the European Championships.
2 Because he's got a fantastic new trainer.
3 He wakes up at six o'clock.
4 His mum cooks for him.
5 He wants to be World Champion.

6 Speaking

Check individual answers.

1 Grammar

a Complete the sentences with the right form of the verbs in the box (past simple or present perfect).

take buy ~~not be~~ not tidy not work build lose come do start see

0 I *haven't been* here long, only ten minutes.

1 You're late! The lesson _____ 20 minutes ago.

2 _____ you _____ the new *Star Wars* film? It's brilliant.

3 Oh no! I don't believe it. I _____ my keys again – that's the third time this month.

4 Jessica _____ her room for more than six months – it's really disgusting.

5 I _____ some great presents for my mum. She'll be very surprised.

6 The Smiths _____ a swimming pool in their garden last year.

7 That's a nice camera. How many photographs _____ you _____ ?

8 Robert Barlow _____ to our school yesterday to talk about the environment.

9 I'm worried about my maths test. I _____ very hard, but I hope I'll pass.

10 What _____ you _____ at school on Monday?

[10]

b Complete the second sentence each time so that it means the same as the first. Use no more than four words.

0 I met Jessica at New Year.

I *have known* Jessica *since* New Year. (know)

1 Lucy and her parents moved to London five years ago.

Lucy and her parents _____ in London _____ five years. (live)

2 Nick became a teacher in 1998.

Nick _____ a teacher _____ 1998. (be)

3 Paul and Luke's last French lesson was last year.

Paul and Luke _____ French _____ a year. (not learn)

4 Amy bought a new car in the spring.

Amy _____ a new car _____ the spring. (have)

5 James played his last football match in 2001.

James _____ football _____ 2001. (not play)

[10]

Grammar [20]

Messages 3 PHOTOCOPIABLE © Cambridge University Press 2006 Module 4 test

2 Vocabulary

Name _____

Class _____ Date _____

a Complete the sentences. Circle the right answer: a, b or c.

0 We sometimes go on holiday _____ Easter.

(a) at   b on   c in

1 Remember to _____ the DVD player before you

sit down.

a turn off   b turn on   c unplug

2 We always go swimming _____ Friday.

a in   b at   c on

3 Did you _____ the CD? Yes, it's on the table.

a take out   b plug in   c turn off

4 Andrew and Amy are getting married _____

September.

a at   b in   c on

5 A: Where can I _____ the television?

B: Behind the cupboard.

a put in   b take out   c plug in

6 If you aren't quiet, I'll _____ the video and you

can sit in silence!

a turn off   b plug in   c turn on

7 I'm meeting Paul _____ eight o'clock. Do you

want to come?

a on   b at   c in

8 Please _____ the coffee maker. The coffee is

ready now.

a turn on   b put in   c turn off

9 Natalie likes getting up early _____ the

morning.

a in   b on   c at

10 They went to Paris _____ see the Eiffel Tower.

a for   b to   c by

| 10 |

b Complete the sentences with the words in the box.

> climbing   canoeing   sailing   snowboarding   skateboarding   surfing   bungee-jumping
> scuba-diving   ~~fishing~~   running   swimming

0 My dad goes __fishing__ every Sunday. Last week he came home with a fish for the first time!

1 I hated _____ at school because I don't like being in the water.

2 If you like the sea, you'll love _____ . You see a whole new world under the water.

3 We went _____ on the river last week. The water was really fast and I fell in!

4 Ellen MacArthur started _____ when she was very young. She went round the world

alone in a boat called *Kingfisher*.

5 I'd hate to go _____ ! Why do people want to jump off bridges?

6 _____ mountains is a dangerous but exciting sport.

7 A lot of teenagers practise _____ in the park near our house. There's a special place

for them, and Charlie often goes there.

8 Go to Australia or Hawaii if you want the best conditions for _____ .

9 I love all winter sports, but I think _____ is more difficult than skiing.

10 To go _____ , you only need comfortable clothes and very strong legs!

| 10 |

| Vocabulary | 20 |

MODULE 4 TEST

UNITS 7–8

3 Reading

Read the text.

ONE OF THE BIGGEST PROBLEMS ON PLANET EARTH TODAY IS THE ENVIRONMENT.

The climate has changed and the planet is getting warmer. We have destroyed large parts of the rainforests and damaged the oceans. Pollution in big cities has got worse. The number of endangered species has increased too. When you turn on the television or open a newspaper, you can often find stories about the environment and its destruction.

Most people think that there is nothing they can do, but it's not true. We can all do something to help our local environment. In many towns, places have opened where you can recycle glass, paper, cans and plastic and, in some places, they will collect paper and glass from your house.

You can walk or take the bus when you go to school or to the local supermarket, instead of travelling by car. Public transport is better for the environment. You can turn off the lights when you go out of a room and you can turn off the television or computer when you have finished. You can save water too. Turn the water off when you clean your teeth and don't stand under the shower for ten minutes! These are small things, but if everyone does them, then the world will change.

There are 'green' organisations all over the world. If there's a local group in your area, why don't you join it? And if there isn't a local group, why don't you start one?

Read the statements and circle the right answer: a, b or c.

1 The planet is ....
   a hotter now than it was.
   b cooler now than it was.
   c too hot.

2 There are .... stories about the environment in the newspapers.
   a a few
   b sometimes
   c a lot of

3 We must remember that most people
   a can do something.
   b can do nothing.
   c can't change anything.

4 The article says we should
   a walk everywhere.
   b use buses if we can.
   c never use cars.

5 You can save water if you
   a don't clean your teeth.
   b have a cold shower.
   c have a quick shower.

Reading	10

4 Writing

This is part of a letter you have received from an English pen friend.

Have you ever tried skateboarding? I've just started and I'm really enjoying it. I go out every day after school with my friends to practise in the park. It's great here because our town has a special place for skateboarders. Do you like sport? Have you started any new sports? Have you got any other news?

Now write a letter, answering your pen friend's questions.
Write about 100 words.

| Writing | 10 |

5 **Listening**  Class CD 2 Track 19

Name _____

Class _____ Date _____

a 🎙 Listen to five people talking about their favourite sports. Look at the pictures and write the correct letter (A–E) in each box.

1 Speaker 1 ☐
2 Speaker 2 ☐
3 Speaker 3 ☐
4 Speaker 4 ☐
5 Speaker 5 ☐

Ⓐ  Ⓑ

Ⓒ  Ⓓ

Ⓔ

b 🎙 You are going to listen to some information about *Madonna*, one of the world's most successful singers. Are sentences 1–5 true (T) or false (F)? Tick (✓) the right answer.

1 Madonna's full name is Madonna Ciccone. T _____ F _____
2 She sings, acts and writes. T _____ F _____
3 She has had ten Number One hits in the UK. T _____ F _____
4 Her films have all been very successful. T _____ F _____
5 She has got two houses in England. T _____ F _____

Listening	10
Speaking	10
Test total	80

Please note that the audio material for the Listening test is on the Class Cassettes/CDs.

Messages 3 PHOTOCOPIABLE © Cambridge University Press 2006 Module 4 test

6 Speaking

a Two students answer your questions.

- Greet Students A and B and ask them how they are.
- Ask each student about experiences. For example: *How long have you been at this school? Have you done anything interesting this week? Tell me about it. Did you enjoy it? How many exams have you done this year?* (You should give examples with the present perfect.)

b Two students talk to each other.

- Explain that Students A and B should take it in turns to ask each other questions with: *Have you ever ... ?* They should use the pictures to help them. If a student answers a question in the affirmative, they should then expand and say when/where, etc.

MODULE 4 TEST UNITS 7–8

1 Grammar

a 1 started 2 Have ... seen 3 've/have lost
4 hasn't tidied 5 've/have bought 6 built
7 Have ... taken 8 came 9 haven't worked
10 did ... do

b

1 Lucy and her parents have lived in London for five years.

2 Nick has been a teacher since 1998.

3 Paul and Luke haven't learnt French for a year.

4 Amy has had a new car since the spring.

5 James hasn't played football since 2001.

2 Vocabulary

a 1 b 2 c 3 a 4 b 5 c 6 a 7 b 8 c
9 a 10 b

b 1 swimming 2 scuba-diving 3 canoeing
4 sailing 5 bungee-jumping 6 Climbing
7 skateboarding 8 surfing 9 snowboarding
10 running

3 Reading

1 a 2 c 3 a 4 b 5 c

4 Writing

Check individual answers.

5 Listening

a

Tapescript

1 I felt terrified when I was on the bridge, 80 metres above the river. I didn't want to do it, but all my friends were watching me. I closed my eyes and jumped. It was amazing!

2 I've always loved winter sports. I've been skiing lots of times. But now I've discovered this new sport. It's more difficult than skiing and it's a lot faster. I love it!

3 My dad has always been interested in climbing, and he often took me with him when I was younger. Now I often spend my holidays in the mountains. It can be dangerous, of course, particularly when the weather changes suddenly. You must wear the right clothes and take the right equipment.

4 When you're under water you're in a different world. I've been to the Great Barrier Reef in Australia twice. For me, it's the best place in the world. The colours are fantastic, and you see some amazing fish, and the silence is wonderful.

5 I love the sea, and I'm lucky because I live just a few hundred metres from the beach. I bought my first board when I was 14, and now I'm an addict! It's my life. I go to the beach most evenings. If the waves are good, I stay in the water until it gets dark.

1 B 2 E 3 D 4 C 5 A

b

Tapescript

Madonna Louise Ciccone was born in 1958 in the United States but everyone calls her *Madonna*. She's a singer, an actress and a writer and many people say that she was one of the most important women of the twentieth century. She started her singing career in 1982 and has had huge hits all over the world with songs from her albums. She has had 12 Number One hits in the USA and ten in the UK and she's the richest female artist in the world. She has also acted in a lot of films including *Evita* with Antonio Banderas, but many of her films haven't been very successful. Madonna has been married twice and has got two children. She now spends most of her time in the UK where she's got two homes.

1 F 2 T 3 T 4 F 5 T

6 Writing

Check individual answers.

1 Grammar

a Complete the sentences. Circle the right answer: a, b or c.

0 You _____ pay for the concert – it's free.

   (a) don't have to   b have to   c should

1 You _____ go to bed so late. You're always tired.

   a don't have to   b have to   c shouldn't

2 We _____ obey the rules in my school. We don't have a choice.

   a have to   b mustn't   c shouldn't

3 What's your bag made _____ ?

   a in   b of   c at

4 School children in the UK usually _____ wear a uniform.

   a have to   b has to   c don't have

5 My new mp3 player was _____ in Taiwan.

   a make   b made   c makes

6 Who was the book written _____ ?

   a by   b from   c of

7 Sally _____ go to gym this week because she's hurt her leg.

   a has to   b should   c doesn't have to

8 Should we _____ an ambulance?

   a to call   b calling   c call

9 I've told you before – you _____ go into my bedroom. It's private!

   a mustn't   b don't have to   c have to

10 You _____ help Ellie with the washing-up – she's really tired.

   a don't have to   b should   c shouldn't

| 10 |

b Re-write these sentences. Use the present or past passive.

0 They held the first Olympic Games in Athens.

The first Olympic Games *were held in Athens* _____ .

1 They built a lot of new houses in the town last year.

A lot of new houses _____ .

2 They play football all over the world.

Football _____ .

3 They didn't make those watches in England.

Those watches _____ .

4 They planted some trees in the park yesterday.

Some trees _____ .

5 They imported that car from Taiwan.

That car _____ .

6 They grow coffee in Brazil.

Coffee _____ .

7 They sell a lot of interesting things in Portobello Road.

A lot of interesting things _____ .

8 They sell millions of CDs every year in Britain.

Millions of CDs _____ .

9 They create a lot of computer games in Japan.

A lot of computer games _____ .

10 They cleaned the apartment this morning.

The apartment _____ .

| 10 |

| Grammar | 20 |

Vocabulary

Name _____

Class _____ Date _____

a Complete the sentences. Circle the right answer: a, b or c.

0 A: I've got some bad news. My car was stolen yesterday.

   B: ......

   a That's amazing!   b That's fantastic!

   ⓒ That's terrible!

1 Do you like my ring? It's real ....

   a leather   b gold   c plastic

2 The film has been a great success. He's a very ...... director!

   a successful   b successfully   c succeed

3 I've got a headache, so please talk ....

   a quietly   b angrily   c loudly

4 A: I only paid £5 for these jeans.

   B: ......

   a That's terrible!   b That's cheap!

   c That's disgusting!

5 A I met Brad Pitt yesterday.

   B: ......

   a That's amazing!   b That's silly!

   c That's crazy!

6 Are you sure that bottle is made of glass? It looks like ...... to me.

   a silver   b cotton   c plastic

7 Wow! Josh can run really ...... !

   a fast   b good   c slowly

8 The images for the early cartoons were ...... by hand.

   a written   b seen   c drawn

9 My shorts are made of ....

   a cotton   b wood   c metal

10 Ben plays the guitar very ....

   a good   b bad   c well

| 10 |

b Illness and injuries. Complete the sentences.

0 I've got bad b a c k a c h e so it's uncomfortable to sit or stand.

1 I feel really s _ _ _ . I've eaten too much!

2 Please turn the television off. It's so loud and I've got a terrible h _ _ _ _ _ _ _ .

3 I'm not surprised you've got a s _ _ _ t _ _ _ _ _ ! You never stop talking!

4 A: What's happened?

   B: Sophie has just f _ _ _ _ _ _ . It's very hot in here – let's open some windows.

5 Jack's having an i _ _ _ _ _ _ _ _ . Don't look!

6 It was snowing last night and I didn't take my coat with me. Now I think I've got a c _ _ _ .

7 Did you know? Paul b _ _ _ _ his leg last week when he was skiing.

8 I've just cut my finger. Where's the f _ _ _ _ - a _ _ box?

9 I often get e _ _ _ _ _ _ when I travel by plane.

10 Matt looks really ill. I'm going to call an a _ _ _ _ _ _ _ _ .

| 10 |

| Vocabulary | 20 |

3 Reading

Look at the texts and the three sentences. Circle the right answer: a, b or c.

1

Libby

I'll be home at 6 o'clock so don't worry about cooking dinner. I'll do it when I get home.

Love

Mum

a Libby has to cook dinner.

b Libby doesn't have to cook dinner.

c Libby should cook dinner.

2

The **Winmouth swimming pool** will be closed until May 10th. The pool in Torgate will be open as usual. Tickets for the Winmouth pool can be used in Torgate until May 9th.

a Swimmers should go to the Torgate pool.

b Swimmers can't go to the Torgate pool.

c Swimmers mustn't go to the Torgate pool.

3

Ellie

Don't forget it's Mark's birthday today. Can you book a table at Luigi's? I'll call Gemma and Sarah! See you there.

Jamie

a Ellie has to book a table at a restaurant.

b Ellie is going to call Mark's friends.

c Jamie is not going to the restaurant.

4

Notice to all visitors
Please be quiet at all times and do not take photographs.

a Visitors should talk all the time.

b Visitors can use their cameras.

c Visitors mustn't talk loudly or take pictures.

5

STRICTLY NO PARKING
in this area between 8 am and 6 pm Monday to Friday.

a Drivers can park in the area at the weekend.

b Drivers don't have to park in the area on weekdays.

c Drivers shouldn't park in the area in the evening.

Reading	10

4 Writing

Name ....

Class .... Date ....

This is part of an email you have received from a new English friend.

> I've just started at a new school. We moved here in August so I had to change schools. It seems OK at the moment. One great thing is that we don't have to wear a uniform! Also, I've got lots of new friends. I especially like Peter – he's great fun! The teachers seem very friendly, but maybe that's because I'm new. My favourite subjects are music and maths. Anyway, tell me about your school!

Now write an email, telling your friend all about your school.

Write about 100 words.

| Writing | 10 |

5 Listening Class CD 2 Track 38

a 🔊 Listen to a telephone conversation between Katie and Ben. Are sentences 1–5 true (T) or false (F)? Tick (✓) the right answer.

1 Katie is calling Ben because she doesn't feel well.   T _____ F _____
2 She has got toothache.   T _____ F _____
3 Ben is angry because Katie can't go out.   T _____ F _____
4 Ben says that she should see a doctor.   T _____ F _____
5 He offers to get Katie some videos.   T _____ F _____

b 🔊 Listen to part of a radio programme with Helen Johnson, a green campaigner. Fill in the missing information.

1 The UK produces more than _____ tons of rubbish every year.

2 Only 14.5 percent of household waste (_____ from our homes) is recycled.

3 Only 5.5 percent of _____ are recycled.

4 Twenty percent of the aluminium in the world is used to make _____ for the American market.

5 If you haven't got any recycling facilities near you, you can start your own _____ .

Listening	10
Speaking	10
Test total	80

Please note that the audio material for the Listening test is on the Class Cassettes/CDs.

6 Speaking

a Two students answer your questions.

- Greet Students A and B and ask them how they are.

- Ask each student questions about their duties/obligations. For example: *What do you have to do at home? Do you have to help with the housework/shopping? Do you think you should do more at home?*

b Two students talk to each other.

- Explain that a group of foreign students are coming to the school. Students A and B have been chosen to tell them about the school rules. They should use the pictures to help them. Encourage them to use the modals of obligation: *have to / don't have to, must / mustn't.*

1 Grammar

a 1 c 2 a 3 b 4 a 5 b 6 a 7 c 8 c
9 a 10 b

b

1 A lot of new houses were built in the town last year.
2 Football is played all over the world.
3 Those watches weren't made in England.
4 Some trees were planted in the park yesterday.
5 That car was imported from Taiwan.
6 Coffee is grown in Brazil.
7 A lot of interesting things are sold in Portobello Road.
8 Millions of CDs are sold every year in Britain.
9 A lot of computer games are created in Japan.
10 The apartment was cleaned this morning.

2 Vocabulary

a 1 b 2 a 3 a 4 b 5 a 6 c 7 a 8 c
9 a 10 c

b 1 sick 2 headache 3 sore throat 4 fainted
5 injection 6 cold 7 broke 8 first-aid
9 earache 10 ambulance

3 Reading

1 b 2 a 3 a 4 c 5 a

4 Writing

Check individual answers.

5 Listening

a

Tapescript

KATIE: Hi Ben. How are you?

BEN: Fine. What about you?

KATIE: Actually, that's why I'm calling. I don't feel too good.

BEN: Why, what's the matter?

KATIE: Well, I've got a really bad cold and a headache and I feel a bit sick as well.

BEN: Oh dear. So you won't be able to come out this evening then!

KATIE: No, I think I should stay in bed and try to get some sleep.

BEN: Don't you think you should go to the doctor?

KATIE: No, it's not that bad. I'm sure I'll feel better tomorrow.

BEN: Well, can I get you anything?

KATIE: That's very nice of you – but no thanks. I've got lots of tissues and a couple of old videos to watch.

BEN: OK then, take care and I'll call you tomorrow.

KATIE: Thanks. Bye then.

1 T 2 F 3 F 4 T 5 F

b

Tapescript

PRESENTER: Good morning and welcome to *How Green are You?* Our guest in the studio today is Helen Johnson who has campaigned for a greener planet for over twenty years now.

HELEN: Good morning. Before I give you some ideas for recycling, I'd just like to give you some interesting facts and figures. Did you know, for example, that the UK produces more than 430 million tons of rubbish every year?! And only 14.5 percent of household waste – that means the rubbish from your home – is recycled. Even worse, only 5.5 percent of plastic bottles are recycled.

But of course it isn't only the UK where things are bad! Twenty percent of all the aluminium produced in the world is used to make cans for drinks for the American market and how many of *them* are recycled? These figures are bad but we *can* all do something. We just need to think more and if there aren't any recycling facilities in your neighbourhood, you can always start your own campaign. After all, we want our children to have a green future, don't we?

1 430 million 2 rubbish 3 plastic bottles 4 cans / cans for drinks / drinks cans 5 campaign

6 Speaking

Check individual answers.

1 Grammar

Name _____

Class _____ Date _____

a Complete the sentences. Circle the right answer: a, b or c.

0 What _____ read when you were younger?

   (a) did you use to   b did you use   c did you

   used to

1 Chloe doesn't know you're here, _____ ?

   a isn't she   b doesn't she   c does she

2 If you _____ very rich, where would you live?

   a are   b were   c was

3 I _____ like mushrooms, but now I love them.

   a used to   b didn't used to   c didn't use to

4 You're coming to my party, _____ ?

   a aren't you   b don't you   c can't you

5 I'd be so happy if Dan _____ me to dinner.

   a asks   b invited   c didn't ask

6 What _____ you say if you met Julia Roberts?

   a would   b do   c did

7 Jack can't drive, _____ ?

   a can't he   b does he   c can he

8 _____ to live by the sea?

   a Did you use   b Do you use   c Used you

9 William _____ be really friendly, but now he's

   so moody.

   a used to   b didn't use to   c was used to

10 You go to school by bus, _____ ?

   a are you   b aren't you   c don't you

| | 10 |

b Put these sentences in reported speech. Use *said* or *told*.

0 Lucy: 'I can't go to Paul's party.'

   Lucy said she couldn't go to Paul's party. _____

1 Natalie: 'I like your shirt, Richard.'

   _____

2 Matt: 'Josh, Tom can't come to the cinema.'

   _____

3 Lydia: 'We've got a new car.'

   _____

4 Daniel: 'I'm busy on Saturday, Alex.'

   _____

5 Rachel: 'Holly doesn't want to go to university.'

   _____

| | 10 |
| Grammar | 20 |

2 Vocabulary

a Complete the sentences using the words and phrases in the box.

> closest friend   argue   ~~kiss~~   get on well with   each other   miss
> have a row   annoy   spend a lot of time   relationship   in touch

0   She said goodbye and gave him a ____kiss____ .

1   I'm very lucky because I .... my mother. We're like sisters.

2   I don't .... with my family because we're all very busy.

3   Natalie is my .... I tell her all my secrets.

4   Do you think Holly and Dan love .... ?

5   You .... me when you don't listen to me!

6   Don't .... with me. Just go and finish the washing-up.

7   Oh dear! I hate it when my friends ....

8   I have a great .... with my grandparents. I visit them every
    weekend.

9   I always keep .... with my friends in the school holidays.

10 I'll .... you – I'll write to you every day!

[10]

b British and American English. Write the missing words.

American English	British English
0 potato chips	____crisps____
1 vacation	....
2	biscuits
3	trainers
4 fries	....
5 store	....
6	pavement
7	wardrobe
8 elevator	....
9 pants	....
10	petrol

[10]

Vocabulary [20]

MODULE 6 TEST   UNITS 11–12

83

3 Reading

Read the text.

Name _____

Class _____   Date _____

Lots of teenagers have heard their grandparents say *'things used to be different when I was young'*. So how were things different? What did they use to do?

Life has changed in many ways in the last fifty years. When the grandparents of today's teenagers were young, they didn't use to be as free as young people are at present. After school they often had to help their parents in the house because, fifty years ago, modern inventions like dishwashers and washing machines were not common.

Not all families had a television, so teenagers probably did more sport and spent more time outside with their friends. Their contact with nature was closer and they were more familiar with different types of plants and animals. Today many teenagers spend their free time on their mobile phone, listening to CDs, surfing the Internet or playing computer games.

You might think that life is better for teenagers in the twenty-first century and, in many ways, it is. But maybe not everything is better ... . Magazines are full of articles on how to look, what to wear, what to eat, what not to eat and how to get a boyfriend/girlfriend. Teenagers want to have the 'right' clothes, listen to the 'right' music and have the newest mobile phone, so it's not surprising that they often feel stressed out ... !

Are these statements true, false or 'we don't know'? Circle the right answer: a, b or c.

1   Older people think life in the past was better.

   a true   b false   c we don't know

2   Teenagers used to have more free time in

   the past.

   a true   b false   c we don't know

3   Teenagers in the past didn't have to help at

   home very much.

   a true   b false c we don't know

4   Washing machines didn't exist fifty years ago.

   a true   b false   c we don't know

5   Today's teenagers spend a lot of time outside.

   a true   b false   c we don't know

6   Technology is important for young people

   today.

   a true   b false   c we don't know

7   A lot of teenagers today go out to

   restaurants.

   a true   b false   c we don't know

8   Magazines give teenagers information about

   clothes.

   a true   b false   c we don't know

9   Teenagers today aren't interested in mobile

   phones.

   a true   b false   c we don't know

10   Teenagers in the past probably weren't so

   stressed out.

   a true   b false   c we don't know

Reading	10

4 Writing

You have been on a school exchange and you have spent a month staying with the Jones family in England.

Write a thank you letter. In your letter you should

- thank them

- say what you've enjoyed about your stay with them

- invite them to visit you

Write 35–45 words.

| Writing | 10 |

5 Listening ● Class CD 2 Track 58

Name ....
Class .... Date ....

a 🔊 For each question there are three pictures. Choose the right picture and tick (✓) the right box.

1 What does the woman order?

 **a**    **b**    **c**

2 What does David look like now?

 **a**   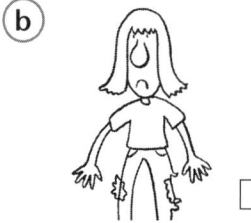 **b**    **c**

3 What are Emma and her mother like today?

  **a**    **b**     **c**

4 Where are the boy's trainers?

 **a**   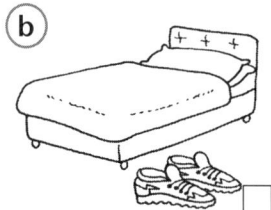 **b**   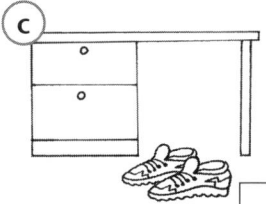 **c**

5 What did the garden use to be like?

 **a**    **b**    **c**

b 🔊 Listen to this answerphone message. Are sentences 1–5 true (T) or false (F)? Tick (✓) the right answer.

1 Amy is calling Liz.   T .... F ....
2 Liz has ordered a book.   T .... F ....
3 The book has arrived at the shop.   T .... F ....
4 The computer system wasn't working.   T .... F ....
5 Amy wants to read the book too.   T .... F ....

Listening	10
Speaking	10
Test total	80

Please note that the audio material for the Listening test is on the Class Cassettes/CDs.

6 Speaking

a Two students answer your questions.

● Greet Students A and B and ask them how they are.

● Ask each student questions about their town/city/village. For example: *What do you like about this town? Is there anything you don't like? What would you change?*

b Two students talk to each other.

● Explain to the students that they have been chosen to make suggestions for improving the local environment for teenagers. Give each student a copy of the prompt card and explain that they should discuss the advantages/disadvantages of each suggestion and then finally choose one as being the most beneficial. (Encourage them to use the second conditional: *If we opened an Internet café, teenagers around the world would be able to keep in touch.*)

1 Grammar

a 1 c 2 b 3 c 4 a 5 b 6 a 7 c 8 a
9 a 10 c

b

1 Natalie told Richard that she liked his shirt.
2 Matt told Josh that Tom couldn't go to the cinema.
3 Lydia said they had got a new car.
4 Daniel told Alex that he was busy on Saturday.
5 Rachel said that Holly didn't want to go to university.

2 Vocabulary

a 1 get on well with   2 spend a lot of time
3 closest friend   4 each other   5 annoy
6 argue   7 have a row   8 relationship
9 in touch   10 miss

b 1 holiday   2 cookies   3 sneakers   4 chips
5 shop   6 sidewalk   7 closet   8 lift
9 trousers   10 gas

3 Reading

1 c 2 b 3 b 4 b 5 b 6 a 7 c 8 a
9 b 10 c

4 Writing

Check individual answers.

5 Listening

a

Tapescript

1 WOMAN: I'm starving. How about you?

MAN: Yes, me too. What are you going to have?

WOMAN: Well, I usually have fish and chips when I come here but the burgers look really good, so I'll have a burger with chips I think. It's too cold for salad today.

2 Is that David? He's changed! He used to have really long hair and he always used to wear jeans with a hole in them. Look at him now – he's got short hair and he's bought some new jeans!

3 Emma and her mother never used to get on well, did they? They always used to argue but now it's great to see them together. They're like best friends now.

4 BOY: Mom, I can't find my sneakers anywhere.

MOM: They're in front of the closet – can't you see them?

5 The garden looks great now with all those flowers and trees. When I was a child there used to be just grass with a couple of trees but no flowers. It's so much nicer now.

1 c 2 a 3 c 4 a 5 b

b

Tapescript

AMY: Hi Liz. It's Amy here. Just phoning to let you know that I went into the bookshop to ask about that book you ordered. They checked on the computer and they think it'll come in tomorrow. They apologised for not calling you but they've had problems with the computer system. Anyway, you can go and get it tomorrow – and when you've read it, can I borrow it?! See you soon. Bye for now.

1 T 2 T 3 F 4 F 5 T

3 Speaking

Check individual answers.

1 Grammar

a Complete the sentences. Circle the right answer: a, b or c.

0 I have lived here _____ 1999.

   a for (b) since c just

1 What _____ your father look like?

   a is b has c does

2 Susan said she _____ to go to the cinema.

   a wanted b want c has wanted

3 If I _____ the answer, I would tell you.

   a 'll know b know c knew

4 There are _____ people in here. I can't move!

   a too much b too many c a lot

5 We _____ television at 6 o'clock yesterday evening.

   a were watching b have watched c watch

6 I _____ come to your party on Saturday.

   a will be able b will probably

   c might probably

7 I think Ben has _____ come home. I heard the door a minute ago.

   a just b ever c never

8 You _____ do that. It's dangerous!

   a should b shouldn't c shouldn't to

9 Harry enjoyed the film, _____ ?

   a didn't he b doesn't he c wouldn't he

10 This is _____ book I've ever read.

   a most interesting b the most interesting

   c more interesting

☐ 10

b Complete the sentences with the correct tense of the verbs in the box.

> ~~see~~ build play give do meet
> not know grow eat sit be

0 It's a brilliant film. I _'ve seen_ it three times.

1 A: What _____ you

   _____ ?

   B: I'm a doctor.

2 Rice _____ in China.

3 I _____ Chris five years ago.

4 I'll get the tickets for the concert if you _____ me the money.

5 Our house _____ 200 years ago.

6 I can't believe we _____ in an aeroplane at 10 o'clock this morning and now we're on the beach!

7 We _____ football after school. Do you want to come with us?

8 Sally says she _____ a famous writer one day.

9 What a surprise! I _____ Jake was your brother.

10 _____ you ever _____ a crocodile steak?

   ☐ 10

   | Grammar | 20 |

FINAL TEST

2 Vocabulary

a Complete the sentences. Circle the right answer: a, b or c.

Name ....
Class .... Date ....

0 A: Jessica, are you OK?

   B: Oh, yes, I'm fine. Don't ....

   a matter b mind (c) worry

1 My brother's so .... – he can't talk to people he doesn't know.

   a confident b popular c shy

2 A: Why don't we go to the cinema?

   B: .... go for a coffee.

   a I'd prefer b I'd rather c I want

3 They're not really interested .... our problems.

   a of b in c for

4 Could I please have a .... for my soup?

   a knife b fork c spoon

5 A: Is Josh coming to your party?

   B: ....

   a I think so. b I don't think. c I think.

6 I've been here since ....

   a the last Sunday b Sunday before last

   c the Sunday before last

7 I need a .... because I've got bad toothache.

   a hospital b dentist c doctor

8 He only wears shirts that are made .... cotton.

   a of b in c on

9 Do you .... well with your sister?

   a go on b go out c get on

10 Goodbye, good luck and have a good ....

   a journey b travel c return

   ☐ 10

b Complete the sentences.

0 I'm sorry I'm late but it wasn't my f _a_ _u_ _l_ _t_ – the bus didn't come so I had to walk.

1 My boyfriend is really g _ _ _ _ _ _ _ – he often buys me flowers and presents.

2 Hannah is very p _ _ _ _ _ _ . She's got lots of friends and everyone likes her.

3 There's a new a _ _ _ _ _ _ _ at the zoo with lots of tropical fish. There's even a small shark there.

4 You should a _ _ _ _ _ _ _ _ . Tell him that you're really sorry.

5 A: What s _ _ _ shoes do you take?

   B: 39.

6 Do you want more potatoes? Pass me your p _ _ _ _ .

7 I went s _ _ _ _ - d _ _ _ _ _ in the Indian Ocean last year – the colours of the fish and plants were incredible.

8 In Britain, if you n _ _ your head, it means 'yes'.

9 Jack and Libby are having another r _ _ . They seem to argue every day.

10 In American English the word for *biscuits* is c _ _ _ _ _ _ .

   ☐ 10

   | Vocabulary | 20 |

3 Reading

The people below all have birthdays soon. Read the choice of birthday presents and decide which present would be the most suitable for each person.

1 Josh loves tennis. His favourite player is Andy Roddick and he watches all the tennis matches on television. He's never played because he hasn't got the right equipment, but he wants to learn.

2 Emily loves the theatre and her dream is to be an actress.

3 Ben likes Shakespeare. He's studied him at school and he particularly likes the films of Shakespeare's plays.

4 Harry has got two sons. He has never been to London and has always wanted to go there with his family.

5 Megan broke her leg in a skiing accident a few months ago. She's OK now but she doesn't feel very healthy. She doesn't like team sports and would prefer to go to the gym.

a Watch Shakespeare on DVD in the comfort of your own home! Enjoy Leonardo DiCaprio in *Romeo and Juliet*.

b Enjoy the sights of London from Buckingham Palace to the London Eye. Buy two adult tickets and the children don't pay!

c Visit Leicester Square in the heart of London's theatre land and go to a show. We have got tickets for *Chicago* and *We will rock you*, the newest musical in town.

d Come to our new gym here in the centre of town? We have lots of classes – from yoga to aerobics.

e SPECIAL OFFER!

Join Sunnyside Sports Centre this month and you can use the basketball and tennis courts for *no extra charge !*

f Everyone who loves English literature must have a copy of *The Complete Works of William Shakespeare*.

g For all future champions!

Buy a pair of trainers and we'll give you a tennis racquet and six tennis balls! So don't waste time, start training now!

h I'm selling two tickets for the **Wimbledon Men's Final. Only £50.** A real bargain, so what are you waiting for?!

1 ....

2 ....

3 ....

4 ....

5 ....

| Reading | 10 |

FINAL TEST

4 Writing

Your English teacher has asked you to write a story called *The best day of my life*.

Write about

- where you were and the things that happened
- who you were with, what they did and what they said
- how you felt and why

Write your answer in about 100 words.

| Writing | 10 |

5 Listening ⊙ Class CD Track 00

a 📻 For each question there are three pictures. Choose the correct picture and put a tick (✓) in the box below it.

1 Which train did Holly say she was catching?

ⓐ  ☐ ⓑ  ☐ ⓒ  ☐

2 Where did the woman leave her keys?

ⓐ  ☐ ⓑ  ☐ ⓒ  ☐

3 Which night is the woman free?

ⓐ  ☐ ⓑ  ☐ ⓒ  ☐

4 What does the man have for breakfast at the weekends?

ⓐ  ☐ ⓑ  ☐ ⓒ  ☐

5 What present does the woman get?

ⓐ  ☐ ⓑ 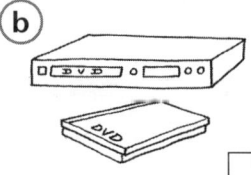 ☐ ⓒ 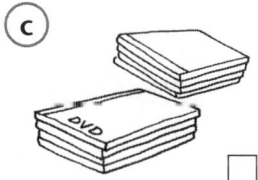 ☐

b 📻 Listen to someone talking about customs in Bulgaria. Answer the questions below.

1 Who invited the speaker to go to Bulgaria?

....

2 What do the Bulgarians take with them when they visit friends?

....

3 What do they always put on their food?

....

4 What do the Bulgarians mean when they shake their heads?

....

5 What should you do when you go to someone's house?

....

Please note that the audio material for the Listening test is on the Class Cassettes/CDs.

Listening	10
Speaking	10
Test total	80

FINAL TEST

6 Speaking

a Two students answer your questions.

- Greet Students A and B and ask them how they are.

- Ask each student questions about what they know about the UK and the USA. For example: *What do you know about the people and their customs? What food is typical? What cities or monuments do you know?*

b Two students talk to each other.

- Explain that they are going to stay in the USA for two weeks in the summer. They should choose where they want to go and what they want to do. The students should use the picture prompts to help them. For example:

  A: *Let's go to …*   B: *Great! We can …*

1 Grammar

a 1 c 2 a 3 c 4 b 5 a 6 b 7 a 8 b
9 a 10 b

b 1 do ... do 2 is grown 3 met 4 give
5 was built 6 were sitting 7 're/are playing /
're/are going to play 8 will be 9 didn't know
10 Have ... eaten

2 Vocabulary

a 1 c 2 b 3 b 4 c 5 a 6 c 7 b 8 a
9 c 10 a

b 1 generous 2 popular 3 aquarium
4 apologise 5 size 6 plate 7 scuba-diving
8 nod 9 row 10 cookies

3 Reading

1 g 2 c 3 a 4 b 5 d

4 Writing

Check individual answers.

5 Listening

a

Tapescript

1 I wonder where Holly is. She said she was catching
the 4.35 train but it's already 6 o'clock and she isn't
back. Perhaps she missed it and caught the 5.35.

2 I thought I put my keys in my jacket pocket but
they aren't there now so I guess I left them in my
shopping bag. I can't believe I'm so stupid!!

3 I'm sorry but I can't meet you on Tuesday because
I'm going to the cinema with Jack. Thursday's no
good because I always go to the gym on Thursday.
How about Wednesday?

4 I always have tea and toast for breakfast during the
week, but at the weekends I have more time so I
have fruit, then egg and bacon with lots of toast,
and a cup of tea.

5 Wow, what a fantastic present! This is amazing – a
DVD player *and* two DVDs. You've been so
generous. Thank you so much.

1 c 2 b 3 a 4 c 5 b

b

Tapescript

I went to Bulgaria on holiday last year because
friends of my parents invited me to stay with them
for the summer. I didn't know anything about the
country and I was very excited. When I arrived,
everyone was very friendly and most of the people
could speak English quite well, especially the
young people. The Bulgarians are very generous
people. When they go to someone's house they
always take flowers, even when they only go for
a coffee. The traditional food is delicious. They eat
a lot of vegetables and salads but they put salt on
everything. Another thing was that when they mean
'yes' they shake their heads and when they mean
'no' they nod – so it's the opposite from what we
do. It was very funny and I often got more food on
my plate when I shook my head because they
thought I meant 'yes' when of course I meant 'no'!
And, one important thing to remember, when you
go to someone's house you should take your shoes
off at the front door.

1 Some friends of his parents invited him.
2 Bulgarian take flowers when they visit friends.
3 They always put salt on their food.
4 They mean 'yes'.
5 You should take your shoes off.

6 Speaking

Check individual answers.

Acknowledgements

The publishers are grateful to the following contributors:

Christine Barton: editorial work
pentacor**big**: text design and layouts

The publishers are grateful to the following illustrators:

Karen Donnelly, Mark Duffin, Martha Gavin, Sophie Joyce,
Jacquie O'Neill, Colin Shelbourne